CACTI AND SUCCULENTS FOR THE AMATEUR

CACTI AND SUCCULENTS
FOR THE AMATEUR

By Charles Glass & Robert Foster

Editors of the Cactus & Succulent Journal

VNR VAN NOSTRAND REINHOLD COMPANY

New York   Cincinnati   Toronto   London   Melbourne

Published in 1977 by Van Nostrand Reinhold Company

A *Division of Litton Educational Publishing, Inc.*

450 West 33rd Street

New York, NY 10001

Van Nostrand Reinhold Limited

1410 Birchmount Road

Scarborough, Ontario M1P 2E7, Canada

Van Nostrand Reinhold Australia Pty. Ltd.

17 Queen Street

Mitcham, Victoria 3132, Australia

Van Nostrand Reinhold Company Ltd.

Molly Millars Lane

Wokingham, Berkshire, England

16 15 14 13 12 11 10 9 8 7 6 5 4 3 2 1

to Vivienne Doney
whose love of plants and warm nature
has inspired so many of us
in pursuit of the hobby
this book is affectionately dedicated

TABLE OF CONTENTS

ABOUT THE CACTUS & SUCCULENT SOCIETY

The Cactus & Succulent Society of America was formed in 1929 in order to help popularize the culture and study of succulent plants and to help bring together collectors from all over the country. In the same year they initiated, under the editorship of Scott E. Haselton, the Cactus & Succulent Journal which over the years has become the leading publication in the world dealing with cacti and other succulents.

The subscription fee for the Journal includes membership in the Cactus & Succulent Society of America Inc., and allows members to participate in all society functions such as biennial conventions. The Journal is published bi-monthly, with 6 issues per volume. The Journal always strives to maintain a balance with material of interest to the beginner, to the advanced collector and to the botanist. Anyone interested is invited to write for further information to Cactus & Succulent Society c/o Miss Virginia F. Martin, Secretary, 2631 Fairgreen Ave., Arcadia, California 91006, or directly to the Cactus & Succulent Journal, c/o Abbey Garden Press, Box 3010, Santa Barbara, California 93105.

Rebutia albiflora from Bolivia, a diminutive plant with soft white spines and lovely, delicate, white flowers.

INTRODUCTION:

Most essays of this nature begin with the question, "What is a cactus? What is a succulent?" We will, in time, get to those questions, but first let's begin with one that is more basic: "What is a cactus or succulent collector?". It is you and we; it is a person who has discovered, or who is beginning to discover the wonders of nature as revealed in a single plant. But why does a cactus, or any other succulent have a grab, a fascination, which for us, admire them though we may, the daisy or the rose or the geranium simply does not have! We do not have the answer to that, for collecting is a form of love, and love is a phenomenon for which we have never been given a complete and wholly satisfactory explanation.

One element in the attraction is undoubtedly admiration: here is a plant which has "learned" through the selection of evolution to survive in what are generally hostile environments, a no-nonsense plant that has done away with all but the bare essentials necessary for survival: some are fierce; some are inconspicuous; few are dainty, delicate or frivolous except in the act of sex, a time when a plant which has spent its whole life

being menacing or inconspicuous suddenly cries out to the world, through an often dazzlingly beautiful flower (the plant's genitalia, as the pre-Victorians called it), "here I am; come and get me!" to the birds and the bees, but also to possible predators. That's pretty wonderful; that's worthy of admiration, for the plant, for life itself!

Another element of appeal may be to the mathematician lurking in all of us. Even if we flunked Math I, we cannot help but appreciate the symmetry, the geometry, present in all of the plant kingdom, but so beautifully obvious in most succulents, in the angles of ribs, the spirals of areoles or nodes; and those of us who made it beyond Math I to geometry or calculus might appreciate the magnificent economy in the ratio of mass or volume to surface area of a globular succulent. What could be more perfect in its simplicity, say, than an *Astrophytum asterias* or a *Euphorbia obesa!* Where in the plant kingdom can one find, other than among the succulents, a plant so simple in its reduction to just one pair of leaves . . . but yet what leaves! These leaves may be decorated with a pattern of windows which provide light for the subterranean production of chlorophyll and storage of water,

The tree in the center of this picture is a pereskia (*Pereskia pititache* from southern Mexico), a true cactus. Though it has leaves and looks very un-cactuslike, the flowers (above right, *Pereskia sacharosa*) have all the typical cactus family parts.

as in the case of various mesembs and haworthias, or, in the case of *Welwitschia,* the relic of a prehistoric relative of the pine tree, they are strap like affairs that just keep growing broader and longer for perhaps hundreds of years, as their tips shred and decay with time.

When you get right down to it, though, the original attraction, more often than not, is that here's a weird looking piece of a plant, which a friend yanked off of his or her plant, which you can just plunk down in a corner somewhere and it'll grow. That's a great beginning.

Back to the question, what is a succulent (or a cactus)? To start with, it's a plant.

Lithops bella, one of the "stone faces" or living pebbles, a windowed succulent of the Mesemb. Family.

That's pretty basic, but it can be overlooked. one subscriber to our journal wrote us complaining that she planted some cactus seeds but all that came up were plants! Second point: what is a plant? It is an organism that manufactures its own food. Zeroing in on the problem at hand, what is a *succulent* plant, it is a plant which not only manufactures its own food but stores it . . . or at least, it stores water, the most essential ingredient of foods, in its stem, its roots or its leaves. Succulent means "juicy"; a succulent plant is simply a juicy plant. What is a cactus? Resisting the temptation to say that this definition gets a bit stickier, let's rather say that it is a bit more complicated, for the cacti are members of one family of plants, so that leads to the problem of defining, botanically, what a family is. A family is a group of individuals all sharing a common ancestry; all people, in a sense, share a common ancestry, and indeed all people belong to the Family of Man. A family of plants is a group of plants which, theoretically, are all descended from a common ancestor, and which, therefore, share various characteristics. The progenitor of the cactus family is generally considered to be a direct ancestor of the pereskia, a leafy sort of plant which to the uninitiated looks more like a citrus tree or a rose bush than a cactus, but yet the floral parts, the reproductive organs of the pereskia are basically very similar to those of all other species of cacti. We will not describe here just what those characteristics are that make a cactus a cactus; there are plenty of books on the subject and they all tell you in detail what those similarities are. Anyhow, if you're that interested you'll want to know a great deal more about the subject than we can tell you on these few pages so write to the Cactus & Succulent Journal for a list of books available dealing with cacti and other succulents. All we need add here is that succulents are found in many families of plants, for, as we already pointed out, succulence is a descriptive term, not a botanical category. There are, for example, common and exotic succulents in the daisy family, the lily family, the milkweed family, the grape family, and in at least 45 other families. So, in short, a succulent is any plant which by virtue of water storage ability is able to survive extended periods of drought.

PLANT NAMES:

It has often been pointed out that plant names are merely handles allowing us to refer to the plants. That is true. It is also often said that God created the genera and species of plants and animals. That is false. We are not being irreverent; God created the plants and animals, directly or indirectly, but Carl von Linne, better known as Linnaeus, created the binomial system which attempts to divide the creatures of the earth into genera and species. In the taxonomically even more confusing pre-Linnean days, one might refer to a plant (in Latin) as "the African aloe from the mountains with very long, plicate leaves that aren't spiney and red flowers" for example; that was more or less the name of a plant until Linnaeus came along and designated the general category of *Aloe* as genus, and the specific characteristic, in this case plicate leaves, as species, so instead of the name "*Aloe Africana arborescens, montana non spinosa, folio longissimo, plicatili, flore rubro*", we have the relatively simpler *Aloe plicatilis*. Bless you, Linnaeus!

A head of leaves of *Aloe Africana arborescens, montana non spinosa, folio longissimo, plicatili, flore rubro* . . . that is, the "pleated aloe", *Aloe plicatilis*.

Plant names, botanical Latin names, that is, tend to frighten many people off, but there is no reason that this should be so; you can find a lot more difficult, hard to pronounce names in the telephone book! Knowledge is a good weapon against fear, and a knowledge of why and how plants are named should make one more comfortable in dealing with those names. We've explained why the plants have names; now as to how they are named

The geometric, globular form of some succulents offers minimum surface area for water loss through transpiration and maximum volume for water storage tissue, such as the sea-urchin-like *Astrophytum asterias* (left) and its relative, a four-angled form of *Astrophytum myriostigma*, the so-called "Bishop's Cap" cactus (right).

Mammillaria theresae, with its dark purple-red stem, white, soft lace-like spines and purplish flowers, one of the best new discoveries in recent years! This is a grafted plant; on its own roots the plant is no bigger than a nickel. (Photo Gil Tegelberg).

. . . that's a longer story. Let us take the actual case of Mr. and Mrs. John Bock of Sharon, Pennsylvania, cactus collectors and rock hounds. The Bocks went on a rock collecting trip to a rock club retreat in a remote and seldom visited part of the state of Durango in Mexico. Theresa Bock noticed a pretty purplish flower out in a field while looking for rocks, and on closer examination they realized that the flower belonged to a cactus, a cactus so small, however, that one would not even have noticed it had it not been in flower, as indeed no one had until they came along. Being cactus collectors, and realizing that the plant was unusual, they sent some samples to their friend, Ladislaus Cutak, an authority on cactus working at the Missouri Botanical Garden. After adequate examination, comparison and investigation, Mr. Cutak decided that the little plant had never been described and named before, and set about the task of doing so. He decided to name the plant after Mrs. Bock and call it *Mammillaria bockae,* the Latin feminine ending -ae indicating that it is Mrs. Bock's mammillaria. If the plant had been named for Mr. Bock, the co-discoverer, the ending would have been -ii, or *Mammillaria bockii,* or he could have named it in John's or Theresa's honor, and called it *Mammillaria bockiana,* or used the plural form, honoring both of them collectively with the name *Mammillaria bockiorum.* He could have named it for the place where it was found and called it *Mammillaria durangensis,* or he could have named it for its long

flowers and called it *Mammillaria longiflora,* except for the fact that there already was a *Mammillaria durangensis* and a *Mammillaria longiflora* (in fact, the latter grows right with Theresa's plant, but that's another story) and there is the rule of priority in naming plants that stipulates that the same specific name cannot be used in the same genus, and if it is done, then the first or oldest name has priority and the later one is invalid. Lad Cutak found that a Mr. Bock, not our John, already had had a *Mammillaria* named for him, so at the last minute he changed the name of Mrs. Bock's plant, using her first name, and called the new plant *Mammillaria theresae.* To indicate that this is the plant described by Mr. Cutak, officially his name is tacked on at the end, so if one is being very scholarly, one refers to the plant as *Mammillaria theresae* Cutak.

To make the naming valid, Mr. Cutak had to deposit a dried, pressed or preserved specimen of the plant at a place that is called a herbarium. This preserved plant is the official *Mammillaria theresae,* or the holotype. Other plants collected at the same time, at the same place, and preserved in herbaria are known as isotypes, and plants collected at the same place but at a different time are referred to as topotypes. If before preserving the holotype specimen, he had cut off a branch or offset and kept it in cultivation, one could refer to that living plant as a "clonotype". But this is all getting pretty technical and away from the point. The fact that one has to face early in succulent collecting is that very few succulent plants have good, universal common names, like "Golden Barrel" or "Burro Tails" and that one simply has to get used to using Latin names . . . and besides that, it can be fun.

The common name, "Hens and Chickens", for example, refers to dozens of different clustering, stemless, leafy rosette plants. "Living Rock" applies equally to species of the Mexican *Ariocarpus* as to various South African Mesembs. "Night Blooming Cereus" is used for everything from *Cereus peruvianus,* a tall, heavy, candelabrum shaped cactus, to various climbing or clambering cereoid plants such as *Peniocereus, Hylocereus, Epiphyllum* and *Selenicereus.* But even aside from the inefficiency of existing common names for succulents, we just feel most succulent collectors would feel more comfortable ordering *Opuntia microdasys* than asking for a plant of "Bunny Ears"!

Just remember that the word genus is singular, genera is plural, and species is both singular and plural. Mispronounce any plant

Kalanchoe rhombopilosa is a fragile succulent in the Stonecrop Family, or Crassulaceae, from Madagascar. The leaves break off almost at a touch, but each leaf roots and with proper care one can grow a plant as beautiful as this one in the collection of John and Mary Bleck.

name you like (it's almost expected of Americans), but never, never refer to "this genera" or "that specie"!

PLANT CULTURE:

Most annoying of the myths that surround cacti and other succulents is the old saw, "they thrive on neglect". Our anwser is that they exist with neglect, but that thrive on tender loving care! While it is true that too generous treatment can kill off a succulent which might have survived for years with virtually no care, to grow beautiful plants one can give far more generous treatment than is generally assumed. We can give you here a few basic rules, but the only way to learn about your plants is to observe them and their responses closely and to be a bit daring and experiment.

Those who have collected for some time have their own potting mix, and they generally are convinced that the use of anyone else's potting mix would kill off their plants. It is true that for those who water less frequently, a heavier, more water-retentive mixture is perhaps preferable, whereas those who water often and heavily or who use plastic rather than clay pots need a looser, coarser, better draining mixture. A general basic mix with which to start would be equal parts of sand, fine gravel or pumice; leaf mold or some similar planter mix; and a loose, sandy-loam topsoil. We use a soilless mixture of just sand

and planter mix, but that means that we have to fertilize regularly and more often.

We also water very heavily, soaking the container two or three times at a go, on the theory that soil cannot be partially wet, but that a little water merely soaks the top layer of soil, encouraging weak surface roots, and

Tephrocactus pseudo-udonis, like its more common relatives, *T. floccosus* and *T. rauhii*, clothed with yellowish white hair, is at home high and cold in the Andes of Peru, but will grow nearly as well by the seashore of southern California.

Coryphantha minima, a tiny, inconspicuous Texan cactus with bright cerise flowers, soon fills a pot in cultivation making a lovely specimen.

that this technique builds up harmful salts in the mix which never get "leached out". We've seen others get beautiful results with far different care, but we're happy with our system, for us, under our conditions, with our soil mix, our climate, our water and our watering and feeding schedules. Experience and experiments will lead you to a system that works for you. The main rule with succulents is that during the growing period they want water, but do not want to be kept sopping wet, so use a mix that drains fairly rapidly and allows a slight drying out between waterings.

There are many other factors which affect culture, and with each there are various pros and cons. Some like plastic pots which take up less space, which being less porous, retain moisture longer, and which are less expensive; others swear by clay pots which allow the grower more control if he has time to devote to his collection; still others prefer the elegant and expensive bonsai type pots which, however, are not very porous but react more like plastic in this respect. As to those who use tin cans, styrofoam cups or plastic dishes, we're not even going to refer to them! We would rather see a common plant which is well grown, obviously cared for and neatly and attractively potted (or "staged") than the rarest of succulents in poor condition and stuck in some old tin can.

Another controversial factor is the use of a top-dressing on the soil in the container. Top-dressings, such as small pebbles or coarse gravel, offer quicker water penetration, slower water evaporation, elimination of a crust on top of the soil, and what is generally considered a neater, more attractive appearance; those opposed to or afraid of top-dressings claim that they make it more difficult to tell

when the plants need water. We feel that experience and the plant's appearance tell you when the plant needs water, but if you don't use a top dressing, at least keep the surface of your mix neat, clean, level and crust-free by "raking" or combing it occasionally.

Most books on culture of succulents tell you not to feed succulents, not to water after repotting, and various other rules that the authors themselves break regularly. Rules are made for those who don't know enough to know when to break them, and don't forget that such general rules have to apply equally to all sorts of conditions and climates. In the hot, dry atmosphere of southern California, for instance, we can get away with techniques that might be sure death for a plant growing in a window or a glasshouse in the northeast. If you're growing a cactus in poor light in a north-facing window in an apartment in New York, you certainly don't want to give it as much food or water as you would if it were growing on a bench in southern California or Arizona!

But the main indication should be the appearance of your plants. If your plants are yellow, skinny or pin-headed and refuse to grow, you're doing something wrong. If it's growing in the shade, chances are, then, that it needs more light; if it's growing in the full sun, and looks that way, then probably it needs more shade. Maybe it hasn't got any roots any more; take it out of the soil and check! You'll learn something about your plants in the process.

We are constantly begged by newer subscribers to our journal for more cultural information along with the plants that are discussed in the magazine. The beginning collector cherishes the belief that for each different plant there is a specific set of rules which, if followed, will lead to successful cultivation of that particular species. In reality it is neither that easy nor that difficult. There is good, general culture which is equally applicable to perhaps ninety percent of the succulents; for the other ten percent, there is some minor variant to fill that plant's specific needs. We find it wastefully repetitious continually to be advising, "good drainage, generous but infrequent watering, regular feeding, light and fresh air", yet for the majority of our plants this is all that needs and can be said. The proper proportions of the above elements is a sense that one develops through reasonable, intelligent, loving care of one's plants and observation of how the plants respond to that care. Some types need a seasonal resting period, others needs more shade or some specific element not essential to other species, and when this is the case, this information should be given, but these are the exceptions. The basic principles of good culture apply to all plants.

PLANT HABITATS:

Knowledge of a plant's habitat can be indicative of the plant's needs in cultivation, but it can also be deceptive, for we cannot know or reproduce the full range and combination of conditions (that is, the ecology) which the plant encounters in the wild or natural state. Competition is a strong factor in the wild, particularly for succulent plants which are usually pioneers in a hostile environment which pack up and move on when that environment becomes too crowded, but because a cactus happens to grow on top of a bare rock in the wild, one doesn't necessarily have to plant it on top of a rock in a pot in one's

Frithia pulchra with reddish purple flowers, another mimicry plant of the Mesemb. Family, like its relative, *Fenestraria* or "Baby Toes", has cylindroid leaves tipped with a rounded window which admits filtered light for the production of chlorophyll inside the leaf.

Many haworthias are windowed succulents, such as the remarkable *Haworthia maughanii* pictured above which has the appearance of having had its leaves cut off with a knife, and the rare and beautiful *H. comptoniana* (below), its leaves decorated with a tesselated or net-like pattern.

collection in the backyard.

We began reading a book recently which started out by saying, "The succulents are found in the deserts of the world. Most of them grow directly on the sand". We didn't bother to find out what else the book had to say. Variety is one of the delights of succulent collecting: the variety of form and color, of intricate pollination mechanisms, the variety of habitat. Succulents are found from the slopes of the Alps to the edges of the jungle or the ocean; they are as common to the plains as to the true deserts. They can be found as pioneer vegetation on old lava flows, hanging on the sides of cliffs or growing on trees. They grow on rocks, even on pure gypsum occasionally, *sometimes* in sand and *as often* in hard adobe! The amazing, wonderful thing is that they can nearly all grow under virtually uniform conditions in our collections!

Mammillarias, rarely thought of as epiphytes, may even be found growing on the trunk of a cycad such as *Dioon edule!*

The hard, pointed, grayish tan tubercles of *Ariocarpus retusus,* one of the Mexican "Living Rock" types of cactus, disguise the plant perfectly among jagged, broken chips of rock.

One of the remarkable aspects of succulent plants is mimicry. This is an attribute which has been developed through natural selection because of the fact that in a highly competitive environment the plants which are seen are often eaten, and those which are inconspicuous generally go unnoticed. Thus lithops, for instance, which are the same color as the surrounding pebbles are missed by predators, and those which are of different colors are soon devoured; those which survive reproduce and a pure strain evolves. Similarly, among the cacti, there are some that resemble rocks or chips of stone, such as the various species of *Ariocarpus;* there are others with spines like grass, such as *Pediocactus (Toumeya) papyracanthus* or *Leuchtenbergia principis;* and *Normanbokea valdeziana* which looks more like goat or rabbit droppings than any self-respecting plant! Many a field explorer has been looking for a particular plant, such as *Ferocactus macrodiscus* or *Ariocarpus kotschoubeyanus,* only to be told, "you're standing on it!" *Ariocarpus kotschoubeyanus* generally occurs in dry lake bottoms and strangely enough, there is a moss or mold in the same area that looks very much like the plant, except that it lacks the symmetry of the arrangement of the tubercles of the cactus. To find this elusive plant one soon develops the technique of looking for patterns in the caked, dried mud. Some cacti, such as the wilcoxias, look like dried twigs, and growing among shrubby underbrush they are nearly impossible to detect except when they are briefly in flower.

Few succulents are as well disguised in habitat as the little "Toumeya", *Pediocactus papyracanthus.* "Papyracanthus" means "paper spine", and the papery spines make the plant nearly impossible to detect for it grows among perfect camouflage, blue grama grass in northeastern Arizona and northwestern New Mexico. The plant shown here (to the right of the nickel) is in bud. (Photo Jim Daniel).

Fine, healthy plants of *Oreocereus celsianus*, a stout, white hairy cactus from the mountains of South America, grown in rich compost in outdoor beds at the Grigsby Cactus Gardens in Vista, California.

PROPER TREATMENT OF MAIL-ORDER PLANTS AND DEALERS:

Those collectors who do not live in the Southwest where there is a high concentration of succulent dealers will undoubtedly be ordering many of their plants by mail. Having operated for years a mail-order nursery, and having ourselves ordered succulents by mail, there are a few suggestions we can offer which may be of use.

There are many mail-order cactus and succulent nurseries which advertise in the Cactus & Succulent Journal, and most of them are good, reputable dealers who offer fine material. They are in the business because they love succulent plants and take pride in their stock. Occasionally plant material is shipped out by even the best growers which is not up to the usual standards; generally if the dealer is informed by a polite letter, a replacement or a refund will be sent. It helps, however, if you know a bit about the nature of the plants you are ordering. If you order what is advertised as a mature, flowering specimen, and if the plant you receive is under an inch in diameter, check first to find out if that species is a true miniature that never grows as large as an inch in diameter before you complain. Realize also that a good dealer is a busy dealer, and few mail-order nurseries can always get your order back to you in a few days.

Succulents are ideal for shipping as most can withstand extended drought. We received one shipment of cacti from South America which was lost in transit and took nine months to reach us, but astonishingly the plants were in virtually perfect condition. Most of the time, however, even succulents suffer a bit from being enclosed in a package for as little as a week or two, especially if they are in an actively growing condition when they are shipped. With proper care, these new arrivals should soon be back in perfect condition.

"Bare root" plants of the miniature *Mammillaria goldii* in flower. Even though the plants are less than an inch in diameter, they are mature, full sized, flowering specimens!

The miniature member of the portulaca family, *Anacampseros alstonii*, with tiny stems clothed in silvery, papery, scalelike leaves arising from a large caudex, growing in a 3½ inch long bonsai pot.

POTTING AND REPOTTING:

Mail-order succulents are usually shipped "bare-root", that is without soil on the roots. If some of the roots are completely dried out or damaged, these should be removed and if fresh root tissue is cut, the cuts should be allowed to dry for at least a day or so; otherwise the new arrivals may be potted up immediately. Always use a pot with a drainage hole, as good drainage is essential to nearly all plants, but particularly to succulents. If it is a clay pot with a large drainage hole, the hole should be covered but not plugged by a curved piece of broken pot, concave surface down, or a piece of wire mesh or screen. Hold the plant in the center of the pot with one hand as you spread your planting mix around the roots. Until you develop the knack for handling even your spinier types of plants with bare hands, several layers of newspaper make a good holder, but for spiny plants such as most cacti we do not recommend gloves for they will soon be so full of spines that they will be worse to handle than the cactus!

One can usually tell by just looking at a plant to what level in the soil it has been growing. Avoid planting it any deeper than it has been growing as this could well invite rot. In the case of most plants the soil level is at the "neck" between the roots and the body. Another advantage of a top-dressing is that the gravel top-dressing can be tucked up under the body of the plant to keep it out of direct contact with the soil. Many succulents grow in the wild with most of the plant underground, as protection against heat and evapora-

tion, but in cultivation they can and in most cases should be grown with most of the stem exposed, both to avoid rot, and so that one can better appreciate the plant. In the case of some of the more unusual succulents with large underground caudices or tuberous roots, most collectors prefer to cultivate the plants with a good portion of the root or caudex out of the soil. Do not fill the container right to the brim with the planting mix, but leave room for watering.

We would also recommend that you select a container which is about the smallest into which the plant will comfortably fit. Faster, healthier growth is obtained by regularly potting plants up into larger size pots as they grow, rather than putting a small plant into a large pot where there is danger of rot through the inability of the plant's root system to make use of available water, and time is lost while the plant attempts to fill the container with roots before it makes much vegetative growth.

If the conditions are warm and dry when you pot a succulent, we feel there is little danger from rot in dampening the soil immediately, and it is beneficial in inducing the formation of new roots. Needless to say, a dormant plant or a freshly potted, bare-root plant cannot make use of water as can an actively growing plant until it has put out new roots.

It is important not to place a freshly potted, mail-order plant, which has been without light for days or weeks, directly in strong sunlight, for even if it is a hardy species which can usually take full sun, it is unaccustomed to it and will be sunburned or scorched. Place it in a light but shaded situation, and gradually reaccustom it to more light.

Opuntia sphaerica (or if you prefer, *Tephrocactus sphaericus*) growing in a shallow bonsai planter.

LABELLING AND CONSERVATION:

Conservation, for a variety of reasons (chief among them, our dwindling natural resources and expanding populations, and national laws and international treaties) is becoming a fact of life to the plant collectors. The days in which we were able to go out into the field and collect our own plants are rapidly coming to an end. The last decade has been a sort of "Golden Age" for the plant collector. The rarest of plants from the remotest corners of the world suddenly became available, even to the average collector for relatively little cost. This "Golden Age" is over, and we are faced with the necessity of preserving and propagating the plant material which now exists in our collections.

At first glance, the combination of "labelling" and "conservation" may seem odd. Indeed, conservation has little to do with labelling, but labelling has a great deal to do with conservation! If plant material is to be of any scientific value to conservation, it must be labelled and documented as completely and accurately as possible. It is increasingly incumbent upon succulent nurserymen to concern themselves with the propagation of rare, correctly named, documented material, and it should be considered a duty of the collector to preserve this information with his or her plants. One should get into the habit of labelling one's plants with as much accurate information as possible. One way to do this is to number one's collection, and to maintain a notebook with these numbers, listing the source

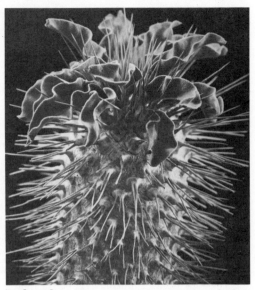

Pachypodium namaquanum is a species which is protected by law in the wild, but has been introduced to cultivation through seedlings, such as the one pictured here, grown from a field collected seed.

and date of acquisition, and as much information about the particular plant as can be obtained. One should get into the habit of requesting of succulent dealers that in the case of documented plants which they propagate and offer for sale, they provide this documentation to the buyer.

By documentation, we mean information about the origin of the plant. Various institutions, such as botanical gardens, receive material which is collected in the wild. Along with this material they receive information about the habitat of the plant. This material should be propagated and eventually be distributed through commercial nurseries to the plant collector. There must be increasing pressure on the botanical gardens, on the nurseries and on the collector to preserve and pass along this information with the plants. In this way, plants which otherwise might be lost to horticulture and botany, may be preserved through our collections through conscientious effort.

Needless to say, we do not mean to say that as a beginning collector your plants are likely to have great scientific value, but conscientious and accurate labelling is a good habit to get into right from the start. One often thinks when one acquires a new plant that one could never forget its name or its source, but one does forget over time and as one's collection grows. The value of one's collection, even to the collector, is greatly enhanced by having as complete labelling and documentation as possible.

Aloe variegata, the partridge breast aloe, is one of many succulents which are quite rare in the wild but common in cultivation. It may be propagated vegetatively from offsets or by seed.

The type plant of *Mammillaria glassii* from which innumerable plants were propagated vegetatively. Now the species is being grown mostly from seed.

PROPAGATION:

As we have said, the ease of propagation of succulent plants is often one of the initial attractions to succulent collecting. It is fun to increase the number of plants in one's collection through propagation and a pleasure to share one's plants with other collectors. Most succulent plants are among the easiest to propagate, either vegetatively through cuttings of the stem, branches or even the leaves, and through grafting, or by growing succulents from seed.

VEGETATIVE PROPAGATION:

The succulent nature of the tissues of a succulent plant enable a small branch, or in many cases even a leaf or portion of a leaf, to survive until it can send out roots and begin to grow again. It is an exciting experience to take a leaf off a kalanchoe, an echeveria or a gasteria, for example, place it on damp potting mix in a somewhat shaded location, and watch perfect little plantlets emerge from the base of the leaf. In the case of branching succulents, we recommend removing the branch one wishes to propagate near but not at its base for greater ease in rooting, then the stub may be removed from the main stem for the sake of appearance. The branch, or cutting, should be set in a dry, shaded location for a week or two to allow the cut to heal and callous before it is placed in the potting or rooting mix. When the cutting is taken, a combination fungicide and rooting hormone may be helpful to prevent infection and promote rooting. In the case of euphorbia cuttings, the poisonous, milky juice should be washed off until the sap congeals. In the case of larger cuttings, they should be allowed to heal for a month or two before attempting to root them. Such cuttings, during the process of rooting, should not, of course, be placed in direct sunlight, since until they have new roots supplying them with water and nutrients, they are subject to scorching and burning. Hardier types are amazing in their durability, and pieces of many types of succulents can lay around for months and even years without dying, and eventually send out roots even when not in contact with the soil! In the case of solitary, rare succulents which do not branch or offset, we will occasionally "top" the plant,

Most plants of the tiny *Escobaria leei* (*Coryphantha sneedii* var. *leei*) in cultivation come from 2 or 3 plants obtained with the permission of the government, as the species grows within a national park.

that is, cut off and root the tip of the stem, which generally forces the base of the plant to put out one or several new stems which may in turn be removed and rooted or grafted to insure the plant's survival.

GRAFTING:

Grafting of some types of succulents, such as the cacti, euphorbias and stapeliads, is a delightfully simple method of propagation. Dicotyledonous plants are those which possess two cotyledons or "seed leaves" in the seedling stage; monocotyledonous plants, such as, among the succulents, for example, aloes, haworthias, yuccas, agaves, etc., have only one cotyledon or seed leaf. In most "dicots" the vascular conductive tissue of the cambium which supplies the plant with food and water, is just under the bark or epidermis. In succulents such as the cacti, euphorbias and stapeliads, the vascular tissue forms a barely visible ring or core towards the center of the stem, surrounded by succulent, water-storing tissue. To make a successful graft with these types, all one has to do is select, for the understock, a robust species of the same family as the scion (or piece that is to be grafted); make a clean, smooth, even cut through both stock and scion (in the case of euphorbias, the milky sap should be washed off, a second cut made and water and sap blotted off with tissue paper); and join them firmly but gently together by means of string or a rubber band, insuring only that the circles of vascular bundles of both stock and scion touch each other at at least one point. The grafted plant usually changes in appearance, being fed by the robust understock, becoming somewhat bloated in appearance and often offsetting profusely, but it does not change in botanical character, and the offsets may be removed

and rooted and will then reassume their characteristic habits. The ease of this technique makes grafting a simple and fascinating hobby or a commercially profitable venture. We know one nurseryman who claims to graft up to 1000 cacti a day! New grafts should be kept in a slightly cool, humid and shaded location until the union has healed and the graft begun to grow. We are not attempting to make you expert or even competent at grafting through this short paragraph, but merely to convey an idea of the exciting aspects of succulent culture and propagation. Again we would refer you to books on general culture which go into these techniques more thoroughly.

A grafted plant of the rare *Pediocactus knowltonii* offsets profusely when grafted and the offsets may be rooted or in turn grafted.

Some species show a greater affinity for one stock over another. Here *Ortegocactus macdougallii* grows considerably more robustly grafted on myrtillocactus (right) than on cereus. We find that young seedlings of *Myrtillocactus gometrizans* make excellent understock for most cactus grafts.

PROPAGATION FROM SEED:

In our opinion, most succulent collectors do a lot of unnecessary fussing about growing cacti and other succulents from seed with complicated techniques. We find that the simplest method, which is basically the standard method for growing most types of plants from seed, is adequately successful for succulents. We simply sprinkle the seeds rather thinly over the dampened surface of our regular potting mix in a shallow plastic container, with drainage holes, of course; cover the seeds with a thin layer of coarse sand or fine gravel; cover the container with glass and newspaper to provide shade and a humid atmosphere, and keep the mix damp and warm during the germination process. Once the tiny seedlings begin to poke through the covering of sand or gravel—usually from a few days to a couple of weeks—we raise the glass slightly to provide fresh air. The seedlings are kept fairly damp and shaded until they are about the size of a pencil eraser, at which time they are carefully removed from the soil (or "pricked out") and potted up separately. In pricking out the seedings, care must be taken not to damage either the tender little plants or their small, delicate root systems. A section of seedlings may be pried up, and the seedlings separated one by one, gently with a pair of tweezers.

From the time the seedlings begin to germinate until they are large enough to be pricked out, the main danger to watch for is the appearance of "damp-off" fungus. If trouble appears, evidenced by seedlings shrivelling up, turning to mush or toppling over, one should immediately remove the infected portion, and move the remainder to a drier location with fresh air circulation. Various commercial fungicides are available to prevent or combat damp-off fungi.

Turbinicarpus species, such as *T. schwarzii* ("polaskii") pictured here, grow remarkably well and easily from seed. It is fascinating to watch the tiny plants take on their mature characteristics as they grow!

One must also be careful in watering seedlings not to cause "wash-out" by using too strong a spray of water. There are various, good, soft-spray nozzles that are excellent for this purpose, or some collectors prefer to water their seedlings from beneath by setting the pans in a bit of water until the soil becomes saturated by capillary action. One can determine the proper amount of light for the seedlings by their color. If they become too pale or yellowish, they are not getting enough light, and if they turn too bronzed or reddish, then the light is too intense.

There is one item we haven't covered, and that's where to obtain the seed: from a succulent seed dealer or from your own plants. To get true, unhybridized seed from your own plants you generally need two clones of the same species. A clone is a plant grown from seed or a piece of that plant grown by vegetative propagation; even a plant grown from a leaf is the same clone. Very often there are factors preventing a plant from pollinating itself, and when such a plant is not self-fertile, it cannot be fertilized by vegetative propagations of the same clone. Even if those propagations were made years ago, and the pieces have been growing independently of each other, they are genetically the exact same clone.

The clones which you hope to cross-pollinate should be segregated from the rest of your collection while they are still in bud to avoid chance pollination. Some collectors use a small artist's brush for pollinating the flowers, but then one has to sterilize the brush before it is used for flowers of other species, so we prefer using just a match from a match book, and a bit of spit, twirl the dampened match in the pollen of the one plant's flowers and then brush the pollen on to the stigma of the flowers of the other plant.

The flowers of *Frailea*, such as *F. castanea* ("asterioides") pictured here, are often cleistogamous and set seed without ever having opened.

Close-up of the center of a flower of *Echinocereus pectinatus*, the stigma lobes of the pistil in the center, surrounded by the stamens, surrounded by the perianth segments. This is an aberrant specimen in that the stigma lobes are somewhat monstrose.

CONCERNING FLOWERS, FRUITS AND SEEDS:

A bit about the birds and the bees is in order! The flower is the reproductive organ of all flowering plants. Its parts are basically highly modified branches and leaves. The scale-like or leaf-like outer perianth segments are the sepals, referred to as the calyx; the inner, often highly colored perianth segments are the petals, referred to collectively as the corolla. Inside the perianth, or floral envelope, are leaves modified into threadlike filaments which support the pollen sacks or anthers; these are the stamens (or androecium) which are the male parts of the flower. Innermost, in the center of the flower is the pistil or gynoecium, composed of one or more carpels, again, modified leaves, the female part of the flower. The pistil consists of the basal ovary which extends into a style and in turn into the stigma and stigma lobes. When ripe pollen is deposited on a receptive stigma, it produces pollen tubes which grow down into the ovary and fertilize the ovules which then grow into seeds. The embryo, with its cotyledon or seed leaves which will provide the seedling with nourishment until it is self-supporting, is covered and protected by the seed coat, referred to as the testa or integument, which has two distinguishing marks, the umbilical scar or hilum, where it was attached to the ovary by the funiculus, and the tiny micropyle, the hole where the pollen tube penetrated the ovule.

At the base of the petals and stamens there are often nectar glands which secrete a honey-like substance which attracts the pollinators, the birds, bees, flies, bats, moths, whatever. In the process of drinking this nectar, they are usually dusted with pollen, and in going from plant to plant and from flower to flower, some of this pollen gets brushed on to the stigma and fertilization may be effected.

This is the basic theme and there are endless variations. If the position of the ovary appears below the base of the perianth and stamens, the ovary is referred to as inferior, such as with roses and cacti, for example; if the position of the ovary is above the base of the perianth and stamens, it is called superior, as in the case of aloes and yuccas, for example.

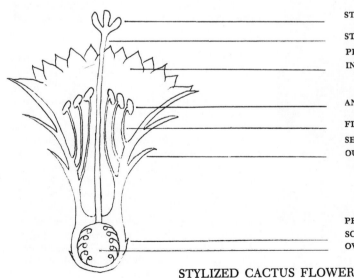

STIGMA LOBES

STYLE

PETALOID PARTS OR
INNER PERIANTH SEGMENTS

ANTHERS

FILAMENTS

SEPALOID PARTS OR
OUTER PERIANTH SEGMENTS

PERICARP WITH (OR WITHOUT)
SCALES, HAIR, SPINES OR WOOL
OVARY WITH OVULES

STYLIZED CACTUS FLOWER

In the case of the highly specialized stapeliad flowers, the petals are fused into a corolla tube. Flowers of the euphorbias are imperfect, or unisexual, in that both male and female parts do not occur on the same flower; euphorbia flowers are also apetalous, that is, without petals, and part of the function of the petals is sometimes taken over by ornate glands or colorful bract-leaves. An inflorescence is a cluster of flowers, and many succulents, such as echeverias and agaves, have elaborate inflorescences. In the Daisy Family, such as *Othonna* and *Senecio*, what looks like a single flower is actually a head of tiny disc and ray flowers (the ray flowers are the ones you pull off to find out whether you are loved or not).

It generally takes from a few weeks to a year for the fruit to ripen. The variety of seed dispersal mechanisms is fascinating. Some, such as the stapeliads of the milkweed family, are wind-borne provided with silky parachutes; some, such as the euphorbias, are ballistic, that is, the seeds are shot away from the parent plant with explosive force as the carpels pop open; some are provided with spurs or barbs with which to attach themselves to passing animals, and in the case of geraniums, such as the succulent pelargoniums, the seed has a built in drilling rig, a coil which when dampened unwinds, burrowing the seed into the ground. Some, such as many cacti, surround their seeds in juicy, tasty pulp, so the seeds may be eaten by some animal, carried perhaps a day's distance from the parent plant, and then deposited in a little bundle of natural, organic fertilizer to help speed the seedling along its way. To get an idea of the wonder of these mechanisms, take just the one case of the spiny, uninviting fruit of the *Echinocereus*.

The electron scanning microscope enables one to see and study minute structures of parts of plants, such as this SEM picture of the seed of the new *Turbinicarpus laui*.

A seedling of the new *Mammillaria pennispinosa* var. *nazasensis* in flower.

The spines protect the inconspicuous green fruit as it is ripening, but when it is ripe it turns a luscious reddish or purplish color, and the spines drop off at a touch, as if inviting the first hungry animal that comes along to eat the fruit and do its bit for ecology and the perpetuation of the species!

As the plant attempts to disperse its seeds, you, as the seed grower, attempt to collect them, picking the cactus berry when it is ripe and separating the seeds from the pulp, perhaps tying a bit of nylon stocking around the ripening fruit of a euphorbia or stapeliad, gathering the nut-hard fruit of the mesembs before they are watered which causes them to open like a flower, allowing the tiny seeds to be washed away, thus deposited in a damp environment suitable for germination.

Getting good seed may take a bit of time and trouble, but it's well worth it for the satisfaction of producing true forms and species, and for the fascination of observing the wonderful ways of Nature! The actual growing from seed is relatively simple and easy and very rewarding.

*   *   *

Unfortunately, experience has shown that one last word on propagation is in order: propagate your own plants, not those in others' collections! Too many collectors see nothing wrong with taking cuttings from other collectors' plants, occasionally even the whole plant, without permission, having somehow convinced themselves that this is not stealing. One hears collectors state with pride that they have never bought a plant, and with great rationalization convince themselves of the self-serving superstition that a piece of a plant has a better chance of growing if you "snitch" it. It is unfortunate for all of us that we tend to tolerate this sort of attitude in our associates, rather than letting them know that what they're doing is stealing.

A brown form of mealy bug crawling across the spines of a mammillaria with mealy bug egg cases in the axils of the tubercles and attached to the under sides of spines (Note black smut fungus on spines), and (right) white mealy bugs and egg cases under the spines of coryphantha.

PESTS AND DISEASES:

The main types of pests which attack succulents are the suckers, the chewers and the rotters! The "suckers", those which suck the plant's juices, include some of the most common pests: mealy bugs, aphids, scale, nematodes and red spider. It has been our observation that the suckers rarely attack a healthy plant, but if a plant is neglected and in poor condition it almost invariably becomes infested. The "chewers", on the other hand, are the gourmets! They generally attack the fresh, new, healthy, succulent growth, and in a relatively short time can devour a staggering amount of plant material. Many of the chewers are nocturnal, and their numbers include snails, slugs, all sorts of "caterpillars" such as cut-worms, inch worms, various other larvae or "borers", grasshoppers and flower-eating earwigs. Constant attention and observation are necessary for effective control. The "rotters" are various fungi, parasitic, thread-like plants, that attack succulents when conditions are right. Most of these fungi thrive in a rather cool and dark, damp, humid environment. If you suddenly find that your plant has turned into a pile of mush, chances are some fungus has been at work. The main thing one can do to combat the fungi is to try to provide the sort of bright, warm, dry conditions that are inhospitable to them.

THE SUCKERS:

Mealy bugs are probably the first pest that succulent collectors learn to recognize. There are the so-called "spine mealies" and root mealies. What one generally refers to as spine mealies on the spines of cacti are usually, in actuality, the white egg cases of the mealy bug, a curious, hairy, little, soft, chalk white to grayish creature which can usually be found half hidden by the wool in the apex or at the areoles of the plant, down in the folds of the ribs or tubercles, or, in the case of leafy succulents, on the under side of the leaves or at the leaf axils. If they are caught at an early stage before there is a heavy infestation, they may easily enough be removed by tweezers or alcohol on a piece of cotton is an old standby remedy; otherwise one must resort to a pesticide with a spreader. A spreader is an additive to the pesticide which will allow it to penetrate the waxy protective covering of the insect; a teaspoon of liquid detergent to two or three gallons of pesticide may be used as a spreader, but preferably, consult your local nursery about pesticides for mealy bugs and an effective, commercial spreader. Dead mealy bugs and their empty egg sacks are just as unsightly, if not as damaging, as live ones. In some cases we have lost good plants, such as various aloes, echeverias, etc., with dense rosettes of leaves, for dead mealy

Barnacle-like scale insects of various sizes and sexes on the tubercles of a *Notocactus crassigibbus*.

pests such as aphids, root mealies, scale, etc., as if your collection were his farm yard. Fortunately there are effective sprays and powders which can keep the ant population under control.

Scale of the type most commonly found on succulents are little grayish white creatures, often as small as a pin head. The female develops a hard, barnacle-like, protective shell, whereas the male appears as a slender little white fleck. They soon multiply and form unsightly colonies which cover whole sections of a plant with their scab-like bodies. Merely scraping the scale off is moderately effective, as once the varmint has formed the scale-like outer covering, it is unable to reattach itself to the plant if it is physically removed, but the drawback of this method is that it is nearly impossible to clean out every crevice, fold, nook and cranny of many types of succulent plants, and the infestation often reappears. Even if one uses a pesticide with a spreader which kills the scale, the shells must physically be scraped, brushed or hosed off. As with any pest, the best thing to do is to catch any infestation at its first appearance.

Red spider, a tiny mite which appears as an almost invisibly small speck of red on or under the leaves or around the growing points of a plant, spins an exceedingly fine web over the surface of the plant. The parts of a plant infested with red spider lose their healthy green color and turn a mealy yellowish gray becoming scabby. Red spider generally only becomes a problem in a closed, stuffy environment such as a greenhouse without adequate ventilation. Sunlight, fresh air and frequent hose sprayings are helpful treatments, but one must catch red spider as soon as it appears or the plant will be permanently scarred and disfigured. Once the red spider is eradicated, the healthy color reappers in the new growth and new leaves.

Nematodes are microscopic worms which invade the plant's tissues. Their presence is often indicated by poor growth and a sickly yellowing of the plant. The most common sort which becomes a problem to succulent collectors is the root knot nematode, so called

bugs, crowded and hidden between the leaves, have caused the plants to rot. One should clean out these areas with a strong spray from a hose and a tooth brush will remove the carcasses from the spines and stems. If several treatments do not get rid of the mealy bugs, check the under side of your benches; in the case of heavy infestations they may even be found hiding out there from where they can reinfect a plant after it has been sprayed!

Root mealies appear as cottony tufts on the roots of succulents which are kept too dry. With our culture and climate we water heavily and often, so consequently the soil in the containers rarely dries out completely and we have little problem with root mealies. When they do occur, most pesticides recommended for mealy bugs are effective used as a soil drench, or one can simply remove the plant from the pot and hose off the creatures with a heavy spray.

Aphids are tiny translucent green (sometimes black, yellow or pink) insects which attack in colonies tender succulent plants, suck the juices and excrete honeydew, a honey-like substance which can cause a black smut fungus on your plants. They go through a winged stage, when they are able to migrate from plant to plant, but generally they are deposited on a plant by one of the most insidious of all pests, the common ant, which tends them and milks their honey as one would tend cattle! One should wage a continuous battle against the ant for, though he does no direct damage himself, he transports and infests plants with because its presence causes a knot-like swelling in the roots of the plant. In milder parts of the Southwest one can scarcely avoid root knot nematodes in the ground, and about all one can do is try to feed the plants sufficiently to make up for the nematode's damage to the root system, cutting off roots and starting over when the damage becomes too great. We use a soilless potting mix, so nematodes have not been a problem for us with pot culture, but if one uses soil in the potting mix, it is advisable to sterilize the soil either by heat or with fumigants to rid it of nematodes. Available sprays for nematodes are non-systemic and only kill the worms when they are travelling through the soil, but do not affect them once they are inside the plant.

THE CHEWERS:

Unfortunately it often seems that the only method of fighting most chewing pests is the old 100% guaranteed-pest-killer-or-your-money-back routine ("place pest on block A; cover with block B and apply pressure"). There are good commercial snailicides for the mollusks (snails and slugs), generally in the form of pellets, but one should also avoid the conditions in which they breed, such as rotting piles of leaves and trash and weeds. There are effective sprays for the other chewers, but it seems inefficient to spray an entire collection when it's often just one or two creatures that are doing the damage, and when once they are detected damage has already been done. It is best periodically to check your plants at night when most of the chewers are active and combat them individually, and try to keep moths and beetles away from your plants so that their offspring in the larval stage will not present too great a problem.

THE ROTTERS:

Few plants are as vulnerable to fungal attacks as are succulents grown in the unnatural conditions of our culture. It is because of fungi, which can enter a succulent through a minor cut or wound, that one is cautioned to heal succulent cuttings until they are well calloused before planting, or to avoid watering a newly repotted succulent in case of damage to the roots which could invite fungal infection. "Damp off" fungus is a major cause of the high infant mortality rate among succulent seedlings, especially those grown in too close and humid an atmosphere for too long a time. There are sprays and powders effective in combatting fungi, but sanitation and proper conditions are the most efficient controls.

We have avoided recommending specific sprays and poisons, but recommend that you check with your local nursery or agricultural plant inspector. Pesticides serve a very important purpose, but they are poison to pests and people alike, and to beneficial as well as harmful insects. Great care, selection and common sense should always be employed in their use. The main point which we hope to have got across is that good culture, prevention and early detection are the most effective means of combatting pests. Don't let your collection get so large that you can no longer give your plants personal attention. You not only lose half the fun of collecting and cultivating succulents, but you're absolutely sure to have trouble attacking a neglected, overcrowded collection.

Buiningia Buxb. is a remarkable and exciting new genus of globular or short cylindroid plants with lateral cephalia—a genus with unlikely similarities to both *Melocactus* and columnar, cephalium bearing types. *B. brevicylindrica* var. *elongata* Buin. pictured here, has small, yellowish, nocturnal flowers.

Opuntia pulchella Engelm., often segregated into the micro-genus, *Micropuntia*, is a choice item for the opuntia collector.

BUILDING A COLLECTION:

There are many types of collections, many directions in which a collector may go. Our main words of caution are not to let your collection grow too large or too fast. If it grows too fast, your interest can burn itself out prematurely and you will miss a lot of enjoyment; if it grows too fast, you are unable to really get to know your plants, and to know them is to love them; if it grows too large, it not only becomes a burden, but you can neither appreciate nor properly care for your plants. Learn to be discriminating, and learn to say "no", a hard thing to do when you're offered pieces of every conceivable type of succulent from friends' collections!

Most collectors enjoy specializing in one particular group or type of plant. Some collectors try to get one representative of every succulent family, or of every genus within a family, but eventually one's interest usually zeroes in on some particular type of plant. In this section we will discuss the various types of succulents, good species for the beginner, and a bit about their culture. Needless to say, we cannot cover here all the major groups of succulents, but we can at least touch on some of the more interesting, popular or unusual groups, and hopefully inspire some new collectors to explore more deeply into this fascinating world of succulents.

* pronounced: pe-rés-kee-ee.

THE CACTUS FAMILY:

Cacti are native Americans. They were discovered along with America, and in all probability were included in the first cargo that Columbus carried back to Spain! They took the horticultural world in Europe by storm, and the first Europeans to see these exotic plants didn't know what to make of them, supposing that they were some strange sort of thistle, from whence comes the name, "cactus". At first only princes and kings could afford to collect these exotic new rarities; they financed the expeditions and owned the botanic gardens. The first plant of *Ariocarpus kotschoubeyanus* sold in Europe brought its weight in gold (and was named in honor of the purchaser!). Today there are cactus collectors virtually in every country of the world. In many areas various species have escaped from cultivation and become naturalized in favorable regions. In fact, visitors to the Acropolis in Greece, to Israel, to Australia or Hawaii often suppose that cacti are native to these areas.

There is tremendous variety among the cacti. The cactus family is traditionally broken down into three tribes, the *Pereskieae*,* the *Opuntieae* and the *Cereeae*. The *Cereeae*, which includes the main groups of collectors' items, is further broken down into eight subtribes or major sections, namely *Cereanae*, mainly the columnar cacti; *Hylocereanae*, vine-like cacti with aerial roots; *Echinocereanae*, low, often clustering plants with flow-

Melocactus melocactoides (Hoffm.) DC., one of the smallest of the 'Turk's cap' type cactus.

Discocactus horstii Buin. & Bred. from Brazil, a marvelous miniature with purple brown stems, gray white spines and large, white, highly fragrant nocturnal flowers.

Coryphantha pulleineana (Backbg.) Glass, a tuberous rooted species originally described as a *Neolloydia*.

Austrocephalocereus dybowskyi (Goss.) Backbg., an unusual clustered specimen of this handsome, columnar, Brazilian species.

Coryphantha potosiana (Jac.) Gl. & F., a columnar species with small, yellow flowers.

Mammillaria mercadensis Pat., a hooked spined species with bright pinkish flowers.

Nyctocereus serpentinus (Lag. & Rodr.) Br. & R., the delicate, highly scented flowers of the night-blooming "snake cactus" (photo Scott E. Haselton).

Mammillaria tayloriorum Gl. & F. from San Pedro Nolasco Island.

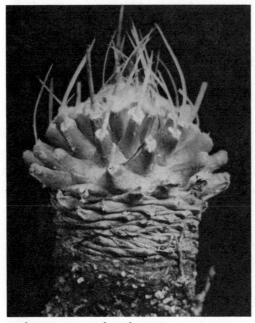

Turbinicarpus gracilis Gl. & F., a new species from Nuevo Leon, Mexico.

Turbinicarpus laui Gl. & F. from San Luis Potosi, Mexico.

Thrixanthocereus senilis Ritt., a lovely, columnar cactus from Peru with snow white spines and bristles.

Cephalocereus senilis (Haw.) Pfeiff., the 'old man cactus' of Mexico is one of the all-time favorites.

Echinocereus adustus Engelm., a rare and unique species from western Chihuahua.

ers from the sides of the stems; *Echinocactanae*, mostly globular plants with flowers from the center or top of the stems; *Cactanae*, globular plants with a highly specialized flowering structure called an apical cephalium, such as the remarkable "Turk's cap cactus", the *Melocactus*, tropical species which bear a fez-like structure of bristles and wool out of which the flowers and fruit appear; *Coryphanthanae*, tuberculate plants whose flowers appear at the base of the tubercles rather than near the tips with the spines; *Epiphyllanae*, mostly spineless, epiphytic plants generally with flattened, leaf-like stems and large flowers; and *Rhipsalidanae*, epiphytic plants with slender, many-jointed stems and small flowers.

The *Cereanae* are an impressive group of cacti, mostly large growing plants which eventually outgrow the accommodations of a container, but for years small seedlings of the various types can offer a great deal of pleasure to the collector. The "old man cactus", *Cephalocereus senilis*, for instance, with its white, hairlike spines, may in time grow to a great plant 35 feet or more in height, but few collectors live that long and small plants of this species are among the most popular of all cacti.

There are many groups of cacti worthy of collection. Even opuntias, the plants which tend to give cacti a bad name with their nasty, little barbed hairs or glochids, which are used for "itching powder", and sharp, barbed spines which go into one's flesh much easier than they come out, even they have much to offer and can make an interesting— if forbidding—collection. *Echinocereus* is another group with marvelous, often highly colorful spination, varied forms and beautiful, showy flowers which makes a fine collection. We have selected for this section what we consider some of the best groups for the collector, either for their ease of culture or exceptional interest.

A large cluster of the true *Mammillaria crucigera* Mart. In habitat the plants are usually found growing in pure gypsum, but in cultivation they do well in most soil mixes.

MAMMILLARIAS:

The "mams" are one of the most popular groups of cacti among collectors, for the seemingly endless variations and forms, their generally small, compact size and their ease of culture. Another factor in this popularity is undoubtedly the excellent monographic study of the genus by Dr. Craig, *The Mammillaria Handbook:* one always enjoys collecting more when one can find information about the plants!

The mams are mostly north American with the greatest concentration in central Mexico. Many are clustering, some with finger-like branches such as the golden spined *Mammillaria elongata*, others with rounded or flattened heads such as the white spined *M. geminispina* and *M. parkinsonii*, or the tiny, fragile *M. gracilis* and the hooked spined *M. yaquensis* with branches that break off at a touch. Some are large, bold, heavy, well-armed plants such as *M. gigantea* and *M. winteriae*, about the size of dinner plates; some are tiny, less than an inch in diameter but with lovely, large flowers, two or three times as big as the plant, such as *M. saboae*,

M. theresae or *M. goldii;* and some, including *M. theresae*, are clothed with soft, feathery or hair-like spines such as *M. plumosa* or *M. hahniana*. Most mammillarias have small but attractive flowers which appear in a ring or crown in the upper portion of the plant, and all are characterized by small breast-like tubercles ("mamilla"), the flowers arising from the axils or bases of these tubercles. At the tips of the tubercles is a spine cluster; the spines may be straight or hooked, short or long, bristle-like, hair-like, feathery or stiff, depending upon the species.

M. saboae Glass, the first of the dwarf mams with large flowers, discovered in western Chihuahua in 1965.

Mammillarias are ideal pot plants, doing very well in containers. The only difficulty we have encountered in their culture is in trying to grow the hooked spine types in the ground. In the wild they usually grow on rocky ledges or in small pockets of soil which dry out fairly rapidly, and they seem unable to stand the relatively constant moisture of the ground over extended time when planted out. With most mammillarias maximum sun is preferable for optimum spine development, but watch your plants carefully and if the stem suffers some bleaching or scorching, then give the plant a bit of protection from the full sun. With a healthy root system and frequent and adequate waterings, most species can take a considerable intensity of sunlight.

M. oteroi Gl. & F. from the mountains of Oaxaca, a hooked spined species which is easily propagated from readily detachable offsets.

Mammillaria dodsonii Bravo, from the mountains near Oaxaca City, a striking species with large magenta flowers.

M. napina J.A. Purp., a fascinating and rather rare species with a large tap root, golden spines and large pink and white flowers from Tehuacan, Puebla.

M. fittkaui Gl. & F., a hooked spined species from the shores of Lake Chapala near Guadalajara.

M. scrippsiana (Br. & R.) Orc., a milky sapped mam from Jalisco.

A dwarf form of M. pottsii Scheer from the Chihuahuan Desert.

M. unihamata Böd. from grassy fields near Ascension, Nuevo Leon; M. weingartiana Böd. may prove to be identical with this species and therefore the valid name through the rules of priority.

Ferocactus glaucescens (DC.) Br. & R., a handsome species with a glaucous blue stem and golden yellow spines and flowers.

F. pottsii var. alamosanus (Br. & R.) Unger, an attractive species from the Sierra Madre mountains of western Mexico, better known by the synonym, F. alamosanus.

FEROCACTUS AND ITS ALLIES:

The barrel cacti of North America, or various species of *Ferocactus* and *Echinocactus*, are another popular group. Though some, with great age, attain a size of several feet and hundreds of pounds in weight, in many cases even small plants are attractive and of considerable interest. Among the ferocacti, *F. pilosus* with its blood-red spines and white hair is choice, as are the lovely, glaucous blue stemmed, yellow spined *F. glaucescens*, *F. covillei* with a bronzed, grayish blue stem and ferocious, heavy, often hooked, ringed, red tinged spines, and the "fire barrel" of the Southwest, *F. acanthodes* with its dense armature of tortuously curved, fiery red or yellow spines. There are many other interesting species, well worth collecting, including *F. wislizenii*, *F. diguetii*, *F. schwarzii*, *F. lindsayi*, *F. haematacanthus*, *F. rectispinus* with stiff, foot-long spines, and the flattened, disklike *F. macrodiscus*, among others. Of all the barrel types, certainly the most striking and one of the best at any size is the "golden barrel", *Echinocactus grusonii*, with heavy, curved, bright golden yellow spines.

F. macrodiscus (Mart.) Br. & R., grows with its large, flattened disks nearly perfectly hidden in the grass.

The ferocacti are by nature slow growing plants. Culturally they offer few problems as long as one does not try to push them too fast in growth. Most species, except for the fat, green *F. pottsii* and its variety *alamosanus*, need maximum light, and they all need good drainage. The ferocacti differ mainly from *Echinocactus* in their scaly but not woolly fruit.

Ferocactus lindsayi Bravo from the Presa del Infernillo in Michoacan.

Astrophytum capricorne var. *senile* (Fric) Okum, a handsome form from near San Pedro, Coahuila, and (right) *A. myriostigma* Lem., the 'Bishop's cap' cactus, with both 4 and 5 angled forms growing together near Jaumave, Tamaulipas.

Closely related to the echinocacti are the 4 species and many forms and varieties of *Astrophytum* which are among the most popular of cacti. Some collectors have large collections consisting of just forms of one species of *Astrophytum!* Of the four, *A. ornatum*, the "star cactus", *A. myriostigma*, the "bishop's cap", *A. capricorne* encircled by long, curving, papery spines, and *A. asterias*, the "sand dollar" cactus, the latter is the most difficult, liking neither "wet fet" nor direct, hot sun.

Similar to *Ferocactus*, but generally smaller in size, are members of the genera *Thelocactus, Echinomastus, Sclerocactus, Hamatocactus* and *Echinofossulocactus* (or "stenocactus"). Of these, one the best groups for the beginner is *Hamatocactus*, as the species, such as *H. setispinus*, are quite easy to grow and rewarding for their attractive yellow flowers with reddish throats. For the slightly more advanced collector, we would recommend *Thelocactus* as one of the more interesting groups of North American globular cacti. The thelocacti are quite striking for their forms and spination, and their culture is not difficult, with the usual requirements of sun and a well-draining mix. Of particular

interest are the closely related *Thelocactus rinconensis* ("lophothele"), *T. nidulans,* and *T. phymatothele,* with large, depressed stems, wavy, glaucous blue ribs with prominent tubercles and, except in the case of *T. phymatothele* which is often almost spineless, stiff, heavy spines which become silvery and shredded with age. We would also recommend any of the many forms of *T. hexaedrophorus* ("fossulatus"), with large, flattened, six-sided, bluish tubercles, and satiny white to pinkish flowers, or the new varieties of *T. conothele,* var. *argenteus* with shredding, silvery spines and pink to purple flowers, or var. *aurantiacus* with orange brown central spines and orange yellow flowers.

Gymnocactus is an intriguing genus, often included in *Thelocactus* but actually more closely related to *Turbinicarpus*. *G. knuthianus, G. viereckii, G. gielsdorfianus, G. horripilus* and *G. roseanus* are of easy culture. More difficult are the lovely *G. beguinii, G. aguirreanus,* and the tuberous rooted *G. mandragora* and *G. subterraneus*. In comparison to *Thelocactus*, the flowers of *Gymnocactus* are small but attractive; the fruit are without scales and split along the side when ripe.

Echinofossulocactus coptonogonus (Lem.) Lawr., the type of the genus, and *E. erectocentrus* Backbg., two "stenocactus" types from San Luis Potosi.

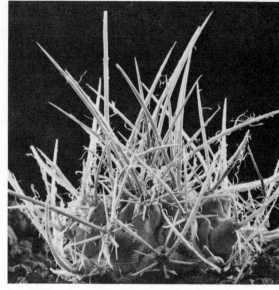

Thelocactus conothele var. *aurantiacus* Gl. & F., a distinctive variety with orange-yellow flowers from Aramberri, Nuevo Leon.

T. nidulans (Quehl) Br. & R., a species similar to *T. rinconensis* but with a greater number of spines per areole.

T. conothele var. *argenteus* Gl. & F., a lovely variety with silvery, shredding spines from Sandia, Nuevo Leon.

Gymnocactus aguirreanus Gl. & F., a soft bodied, spiney plant with fleshy roots and small yellow flowers from the Sierra de la Paila in Coahuila.

T. rinconensis (Pos.) Br. & R., generally mislabeled in collections as *T. lophothele,* a striking blue bodied species from near Saltillo, Coahuila.

G. beguinii var. *senilis* (Hort.) a spectacular, long spined variety of this attractive species from near Saltillo.

Ariocarpus agavoides (Casteñ.) Anderson, a small species with long, leathery, strap-like tubercles and deep magenta flowers, is so distinct that it was first described as a new genus, *Neogomesia*. It grows well concealed on dusty, rocky hillsides near Tula, Tamaulipas.

Ariocarpus kotschoubeyanus (Lem.) K. Schumann (below), from the Chihuahuan Desert of northern Mexico.

LIVING ROCK CACTI:

Among the most unusual of the cacti, and highly prized among collectors, are the many types which may be referred to as "living rock" cacti. They are slow growing cacti from the arid Chihuahuan Desert of northern central Mexico and southern Texas with rather rough, wrinkled or fissured, rock-like bodies which are inconspicuous and well disguised in their generally rocky habitats. The main genus of "living rocks" is *Ariocarpus,* tuberculate plants with mammillaria-like fruit: *A. fissuratus* with deeply fissured tubercles and rose colored flowers, the one species which occurs in Texas; *A. retusus,* with short, pointed, pyramidal, often wrinkled, usually grayish brown tubercles and white or occasionally pink flowers; *A. trigonus* with elongated pyramidal, incurved, clawlike, grayish green tubercles and yellow flowers; *A. kotschoubeyanus* with small, flat, pointed, woolly tubercles in a mosaic pattern and magenta or occasionally white flowers; or the rare *A. scapharostrus* and *A. agavoides,* with long, rough, leathery tubercles and deep magenta flowers. Here the usual requirements of a well draining potting mix, a warm, sunny location and infrequent waterings are particularly important as these species are all exceedingly slow growing plants and cannot be pushed.

Plants of similar appearance and culture which are appropriate in a collection of "living rocks" include such types as *Obregonia denegrii,* a plant shaped like a broad, flattened pine cone, with greenish gray to brownish, S-shaped, pyramidal, pointed tubercles, short, curved spines and small, white flowers, which grows in the sun in habitat, but which generally prefers some shade in cultivation; *Strombocactus disciformis,* top- or turnip-shaped plants with flattened heads, low, rasty, bluish tubercles with white spines only near

Ariocarpus fissuratus (Engelm.) K. Schumann, with fissured tubercles resembling the weathered rocks among which it often grows, is sometimes separated into the genus *Roseocactus,* along with *A. kotschoubeyanus,* because of its grooved tubercles.

Aztekium ritteri (Böd.) Böd. from canyon walls in Nuevo Leon is one of the great oddities of the cactus family. It was named to honor the Aztec Indians of Mexico. With reasonable care it does surprisingly well in cultivation. *Obregonia denegrii* Fric (right) is another most peculiar monotypic genus from Tamaulipas, Mexico. Young plants of obregonia grown from seed are most attractive, looking like little, dark-green sempervivums!

the center of the stem, and white flowers, a species which grows in the wild on low, dry, dusty, shale ridges in the state of Queretaro, Mexico; *Aztekium ritteri*, a unique, fantastic little plant, its rounded, depressed, bluish stem completely covered with furrows and sagging ridges, and small, apical, whitish flowers which are quite uncactuslike with but few petals or perianth segments; and *Pelecyphora*, a remarkable genus with just two species: *P. aselliformis* with rounded, depressed stems covered with brownish gray, truncate, hatchet-shaped tubercles with tiny, flattened, appressed spines and beautiful magenta and pink flowers, and *P. strobiliformis* ("encephalocarpus") with stems shaped like tight broad cones of a conifer with flattened, imbricated, tannish tubercles and flowers like those of *P. aselliformis*. Originally included in *Pelecyphora*, the two species of *Normanbokea* fit into this group aesthetically if not botanically, *N. valdeziana*, tiny, spher-

ical bodies with tiny spine clusters of feathery, lace-like spines and magenta to white flowers, and *N. pseudopectinata*, with small, depressed stems similar to those of *P. aselliformis* except for the more prominent, white, appressed spines and the white to magenta flowers.

Closely related to *Normanbokea*, though different in appearance, are the various species of *Turbinicarpus*, at one time included in *Strombocactus*. These are little plants with brownish or blue-green turnip-shaped stems and papery to hair-like spines, inconspicuous little plants which do very well in cultivation and grow like weeds from seed. We can readily recommend any of the species such as *T. schmiedickeanus*, *T. macrochele*, *T. schwarzii*, *T. klinkerianus*, *T. lophophoroides*, *T. pseudomacrochele* or the new *T. laui*.

These "living rock" types are among the most outlandish of all cacti, of all plants for that matter, and though they are mostly not the easiest to cultivate, no collection should

Pelecyphora aselliformis Ehrenberg from San Luis Potosi is one of the most irresistably fascinating of Mexican "living rock" type cacti! To the native Mexicans it shares with *Lophophora* the name "peyote". *P. strobiliformis* (Werd.) Fric & Schelle (right) is generally known under Berger's generic name "Encephalocarpus" but it is floristically very closely related to *P. aselliformis*.

Epithelantha micromeris (Eng.) Web., the little "button cactus", has many forms, such as the attractive cluster pictured here from northwest of Monterrey, Coahuila.

be without at least one or two of them.

Epithelantha is a really neat little genus of small, white, pebble-like, solitary or clustering plants often called "button cactus". The spines are so tiny and dense that they give the plant an almost smooth, white appearance; the flowers are small and pink and the fruits are elongated, fleshy and bright red. The plants need a particularly loose mix and should not be kept too wet.

"Peyote" or *Lophophora* should be mentioned in passing as it is usually associated with this group. To many Indians of North America the "peyote" has been considered a sacred plant, a part of God, and in ritual these plants are eaten, not unsimilarly to the sacrament of communion in some Christian religions, and the consumption of peyote has a hallucinogenic effect usually producing color visions. Because of the drug-like content of these plants, most of us are not permitted by law to possess them in our collections, an unfortunate restriction for what cactus collector is going to eat his plants (besides that, the taste is nauseous!). It is a shame that *Lophophora* is outlawed, too, for it is a most singular little plant with a soft, fleshy, bluish body and spineless areoles with copious tufts of soft, white wool, a pretty plant which looks good enough to eat!

Turbinicarpus schmiedickeanus (Böd.) Buxb. & Backbg. from Tamaulipas is the first member of this peculiar genus to have been discovered. *Normanbokea valdeziana* (Möll.) Klad. & Buxb. (right) is a curious little plant with feathery, lace-like spines and magenta to whitish flowers.

Sclerocactus polyancistrus (Eng. & Big.) Br. & R. from the barren Mojave Desert is a lovely plant with brown and white spines and delicate magenta flowers but it has little hope of surviving in captivity.

THE DIFFICULT CACTI
OF THE AMERICAN SOUTHWEST:

The deserts of the southwestern United States are among the most severe habitats for cacti, and the highly specialized plants which survive there are among the most difficult to cultivate. Few plants are as ephemeral in collections as are various species of *Sclerocactus* or *Pediocactus*. In the wild these species are rare and among the more endangered, and every effort should be made to preserve them both in the natural state and in cultivation, but that is no easy task for even the most experienced cactus growers, even those who live in areas where these plants occur, have difficulty keeping them alive in collections. The plants simply cannot take the more generous conditions of unnatural cultivation. A few growers have had some success by giving the touchy ones, such as *Pediocactus bradyi, P. paradinei, P. papyracanthus, P. fickeiseniae, P.* ("utahia") *sileri* or *Sclerocactus* ("coloradoa") *mesae-verdae* a completely dry, long and cool resting period throughout the fall, winter and early spring. We have had the greatest success by grafting the plants, thus forcing them to offset, then removing the offsets and rooting them, through which process they seem better able to cope with cultivation. These plants are great oddities deserving special efforts. Few cacti are more beautiful than a perfect plant of *Pediocactus paradinei* with long, silvery white, hairlike spines, or more unique than *P. papyracanthus*, hidden by papery, grass-like spines, or *P. fickeiseniae* with strange, coarse, cardboard-like spines.

Pediocactus paradinei B.W. Benson, is one of the loveliest of North American cacti in habitat but all too ephemeral in collections.

Sulcorebutia krahnii Rausch is a most attractive species with straight, golden spines and golden yellow flowers.

SOUTH AMERICAN GLOBULAR CACTI:

Among the best groups for the beginner, for their ease of culture, beautiful form and spination, and easy flowering, are some of the South American genera of globular cacti, particularly members of *Rebutia, Sulcorebutia, Gymnocalycium* and *Notocactus*. The more advanced will also be attracted to such groups as *Copiapoa, Neoporteria, Parodia, Frailea, Matucana* and *Oroya*, which take a bit more specialized care.

Rebutias are small, globular, profusely clustering plants with highly colored, large, very attractive flowers which arise in a ring around the base of the plant often forming a crown of flowers around each stem. Old favorites are *Rebutia minuscula* with tiny, bristly spines and deep red flowers, and *R. senilis* with long, glassy white spines and blood-red flowers. Similar to the latter and strikingly beautiful is *R. muscula* with dense, white spines and deep orange flowers. Among the choicest are *R. heliosa*, a relatively new species with a dense covering of short, pectinate, silvery gray spines and slender reddish orange flowers, or the delicate *R. albiflora* with small, delicate stems, hair-like spines and pure white flowers. Some of the rebutias are occasionally separated into the genus *Aylostera*, but this is generally just considered a sub-group of *Rebutia*. Every rebutia is a delight and well worth cultivating. Too intense sunlight should be avoided, but otherwise they are of the easiest culture.

Similar in appearance and habit to the rebutias, but with more variety of form and spination, are the sulcorebutias. Not very long ago the only known species of *Sulcorebutia* was S. *steinbachii* with dark, spider-like spines and rich purplish flowers, but recently a wealth of new species has been

Sulcorebutia crispata Rausch, another excellent, little, clustering species with curly, appressed spines and purple flowers.

Sulcorebutia rauschii Frank is perhaps the best of the newer sulcos, with a velvety, reddish purple stem, tiny black spines and magenta flowers.

discovered by field explorers in the remoter parts of Bolivia. Among the most exciting of the new discoveries is S. *rauschii*, the small, round stems a bluish purple in color and of an almost velvety texture, with short, appressed, jet-black spines and rich reddish purple flowers, a real jewel of a plant! Nearly all sulcos are worthy of note, but among the best are S. *krahnii* with bristly orange-yellow spines and yellow flowers, S. *arenacea* with dark brown bodies, short, pectinate, snow-white spines and yellow flowers, S. *candiae* with chocolate brown stems and golden yellow spines and flowers, S. *menesesii* with purple-brown stems and tortuous spines, and S. *crispata* with curly, appressed yellowish to brownish spines and reddish purple flowers. The sulcos are generally characterized by low, rounded, but prominent tubercles and a linear, groove-like areole; the flowers are similar in appearance to those of *Rebutia*.

Rebutia heliosa Rausch, another superlative plant with silver-gray, appressed spines and slender orange flowers.

The gymnocalyciums, or "chin cacti", are another excellent group for the beginner or advanced collector. They are characterized by a naked flower and fruit which bear scales but no hair or wool, and by chin-like protuberances below each areole and spine cluster. They offer great variety of form, spination, flower and color. Among the most noteworthy would be *Gymnocalycium denudatum* with a smooth, shiny green, bulging stem and completely appressed, flattened, yellowish, spider-like spine clusters, G. *bruchii* forming large clusters of small, bluish stems with short, curly appressed, white spines and pink flowers, G. *saglione*, the largest of the genus, with fat, rounded tubercles, stiff, reddish golden, arching spines, and short, broad, flesh colored flowers, and G. *mihanovichii* with its many varieties, including the fascinating, highly popular "ruby ball" cultivar, a horticultural oddity which lacks chlorophyll and must be grown grafted. For the advanced collector there are wonderful novelties such as G. *pseudo-malacocarpus*, G. *griseopallidum*, G. *cardenasianum*, G. *castellanosii* and the rare G. *spegazzinii*, among many other wonderful selections!

Gymnocalycium denudatum (Lk. & O.) Pfeiff., "spider cactus", is a marvel even of the cactus world with a smooth, wax-like, dark green body and appressed, spider-like spine clusters.

Gymnocalycium spegazzinii Br. & R. is one of the choicest items of this popular genus. *Notocactus buiningii* Buxb. (right) is a most handsome Brazilian species of the "malacocarpus" type.

Gymnocalycium saglione (Cels) Br. & R., the "giant chin cactus", is the largest of the genus, imposing and easy to grow.

Copiapoa cinerea (Phil.) Br. & R., a marvelous species of this Chilean genus with stout black spines, and an ashy grayish white body, the texture of weathered shoe leather.

Gymnocalycium pseudo-malacocarpus Backbg. is an interesting species from Bolivia with a bronzed, olive-green stem and wrinkled, angular ribs.

Copiapoa hypogaea Ritt., a curious plant with wrinkled, chocolate brown stems, black spines and bright yellow flowers.

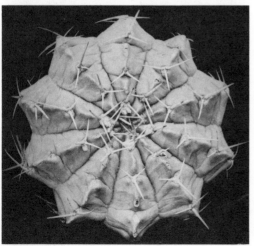

Borzicactus madisoniorum P.C. Hutch., an intriguing "matucana" type plant from Peru with slender, deep red flowers.

Parodia uhligiana Backeberg from Argentina is a highly attractive species with brown and white spines and wine red flowers.

Notocactus leninghausii (Haage Jr.) Berg. is deservedly one of the most popular of cacti, forming clusters of golden spined, yellow flowered columns with whimsically tilted tops.

Notocactus crassigibbus Ritt. superficially looks more like a gymnocalycium until one sees the flowers clothed in wool.

Notocactus magnificus (Ritt.) Krainz from Brazil well deserves its name with its bluish body, golden spines and flowers.

Neochilenia aerocarpa var. *fulva* (Ritt.) Backbg., a handsome variety with brownish stems, black spines and carmine flowers, from Chile. Right: *Matucana haynei* (O.) Br. & R., a lovely species.

Species of *Notocactus* are undoubtedly the best plants for the beginner, and one never tires of their beautiful spination and flowers. The notocactus flowers are usually large and of a lovely, satiny sheen, generally bright yellow though occasionally peach, cerise, and even into the purple shades; many are characterized by reddish purple stigma lobes. Few cacti can top such favorites as *Notocactus haselbergii* with bristly white spines and rather small, crimson flowers that last for up to three weeks, *N. leninghausii*, a columnar, clustering species with soft golden spines, a whimsically tilted apex and large, pure yellow flowers, or *N. scopa* with brush-like clusters of white to silvery gray and reddish spines and large yellow flowers. Among the collector's items are *N. crassigibbus*, *N. buiningii*, and the appropriately named *N. magnificus*.

Virtually none of the members of these four genera, *Rebutia, Sulcorebutia, Gymnocalycium,* and *Notocactus* are the least bit picky. All they need are the usual requirements of a fairly rich but well-drained soil or planting mix, generous waterings when the growing medium starts to dry out, and a bright, airy location.

Uebelmannia pectinifera Buin. is one of the most startling new discoveries in the world of cacti in recent years. This handsome species with its neat rows of comb-like spines, small yellow flowers and rough textured stems flecked with white scales, more resembles an astrophytum than any other Brazilian cactus.

Notocactus nigrispinus (K. Schum.) Buin., an "eriocactus" type, similar to *N. leninghausii, N. claviceps* and *N. schumannianus,* but with long, stiff dark spines.

Colorful "orchid cactus", hybrids of *Epiphyllum*, are spectacular for color, size and shape of the flowers. The graceful branches are flattened, green and leaf-life from whence we get the name "epiphyllum" or "out of the leaf", implying erroneously that they flower from the leaves! There are innumerable beautiful hybrid "orchid cactus" from which to choose.

EPIPHYTIC CACTI AND NIGHT BLOOMING CEREUS:

The epiphytic cacti, that is, those which grow on the bark or branches of trees rather than in the ground, are a specialized group which is virtually a field of its own, requiring quite different care from most other succulents. The epiphytes, consisting mainly of *Epiphyllum*, *Schlumbergera* ("zygocactus"), *Rhipsalis* and related genera, want light shade, and exceedingly loose and humusy, well draining potting mix and frequent sprayings as well as waterings and feedings. Fuchsia, begonia and fern growers often have greater success than cactus collectors in growing beautiful specimens of epiphytic cacti!

The true epiphyllums are "night blooming cereus" in the sense that they are members of the *Cereeae* tribe with white flowers which open at night. What we commonly refer to as "epiphyllums" are the hybrid "orchid cacti", epiphyllums which have been crossed with cacti with large, colorful, day-blooming flowers. Members of the *Hylocereanae*, such as *Hylocereus* and *Selenicereus* with large, spectacularly beautiful, nocturnal flowers, are also sometimes called night-blooming cereus. These plants are epiphytic climbers, with undulate, triangular or rounded, spiny stems, and aerial roots. They may be trained to climb posts or tree trunks. Large columnar or candelabriform members of the genus *Cereus* are also night flowering and may reasonably be considered "night blooming cereus".

Species and cultivars of *Schlumbergera* ("zygocactus", "Christmas cactus", etc.), like the orchid cacti, have lovely, colorful flowers. The flowers are zygomorphic (that is, not radially symmetrical, and the branchlets are often delicate little affairs, reminiscent of the legs of crabs. A large, old plant of "Christmas cactus" in bloom is a spectacular sight indeed!

The rhipsalis are a neglected group of cacti highly deserving of cultivation. The flowers are small and individually inconspicuous, but a spray of rhipsalis in full flower is a charming sight with hundreds of delicate little flowers all along the branchlets. Rhipsalis are graceful, hanging plants, intricate in form and tropical in quality. Among the more interesting species, *Rhipsalis heteroclada*, *R. mesembryanthemoides*, *R. paradoxa*, and *R. pachyptera* with flattened, leaf-like, crenate, purplish branches, are particularly to be recommended.

Schlumbergera truncata (Haw.) Moran and its hybrids, often referred to as "zygocactus", "Christmas cactus" or "Grandmother's cactus", are particularly desirable for their beautiful flowers and graceful habit.

Rhipsalis heteroclada Br. & R. from Brazil is a lovely, graceful species deserving cultivation.

OTHER SUCCULENTS:

As we said, succulents occur (or succulence occurs) in many families of plants other than the cactus family. Cactus is such a popular group of succulent plants that succulents other than cacti are often referred to as "other succulents". Common usage is the only reason why these marvelous other succulents should have to take second place! Jacobsen covers the field of other succulents in his exceptional work, *A Handbook of Succulent Plants*, in three volumes; in the next few pages we will give you at least a taste of some of the more interesting of the other succulents.

AGAVE AND ITS ALLIES:

Like the cacti, agaves are purely American plants, and like the cacti they have become naturalized in various parts of the world, such as Africa and along the Riviera in southern France. Commercially the agave is probably one of the most important of succulents. Its fibers are used to make rope such as sisal, a strong white rope made from *Agave sisalana*, or coarse "istle" from *Agave lecheguilla*, and its sap is distilled to make mescal such as Tequila from *Agave tequilana*. When the agave is about to flower, its sap becomes quite sugary and may be collected as "agua miel", or honey-water, which may be fermented to make "Pulque", a popular drink in Mexico since pre-Columbian times. The skin of the agave used to be used as paper, the spines as needles and the roots to make yellow dye; even the leaves are used as a crude sort of tile to thatch roofs. The plants themselves are not only decorative, but are used as effective hedges and fences.

The agaves are monocarpic, that is, after flowering the plant dies; in the case of clustering types, the head that flowers dies. The plant virtually expends itself on the production of the massive terminal inflorescence. "Agave" means "noble", and could refer equally well to the elegant shape of the plant with its graceful leaves as to the impressive and stately flowers stalk.

Agaves are grown for their fiber and for pulque, among other uses, in fields such as this one outside Mexico City.

Agaves, such as *A. tequilana*, are harvested, the leaves removed and the hearts roasted, after which the juice is distilled into mescal, such as Tequila (below).

We find the agave subject to few pests. There is a borer, a larva which can burrow into the leaves and attack the heart of the plant, but even this creature serves a purpose; in Mexico it is known as an agave worm, or "guzano de maguey", and is considered a delicacy when roasted or powdered and eaten with mescal, a fitting fate!

Larger agaves, such as *Agave americana*, *A. ferox* or *A. franzosini*, all with leaves often over six feet long, may be effectively used in landscaping, as may smaller types such as the elegant *Agave victoriae-reginae*, *A. pattonii* ("huachucensis") or *A. vilmoriniana*, but the even smaller, dwarf types make ideal pot plants such as *Agave parviflora* with leaves often only an inch or two long, striped with white and with coarse white threads along the margins of the leaves, *Agave utahensis*, a hardy type with narrow, gray-blue leaves with long, handsome terminal spines, or the highly prized miniatures, *Agave filifera* var. *compacta*, and *A. pumila*, a stunted form of *A. lophantha*. Of all the various agaves, however, none is more regal or striking in appearance than *Agave victoriae-reginae* with its artichoke-like rosette of dark green leaves striped with patterns of white and tipped with pitch-black, terminal spines!

One of the striking features of agaves is the beautiful and intricate pattern of the leaves which are imprinted or "embossed" on the neighboring leaves when they are tightly pressed together as they emerge from the

An attractive form of *Agave patonii* Trel., frequently misidentified as *A. huachucensis*, from Durango, Mexico.

Agave utahensis Engelm. is a striking, hardy species, with its many forms, such as the long spined variety *nevadensis* pictured here.

heart or "bud" of leaves. This characteristic has been dubbed "bud-printing".

We are fortunate to have various reference books available on *Agave*, such as *The Agave Family in Sonora* by Gentry and *The Agaves* by Breitung, dealing with comonly cultivated species.

Agave parviflora Torr. is undoubtedly the smallest of the dwarf agaves often with leaves hardly an inch long! The stiff, dark green leaves have white markings and coarse marginal hairs.

RELATIVES OF THE AGAVES:

There are several groups of Mexican plants which have been shuffled back and forth between the lily family, the amaryllis family and the agave family. We're not particularly concerned with their taxonomic position here, but with their culture and value to the collector. Among them are the genera *Yucca, Beaucarnea, Nolina,* and *Calibanus.* Most of these types are too large growing for a potted collection but ideal for landscaping in milder areas. Two of the finest arborescent yuccas are *Y. filifera* with rosettes of dark green leaves with coarse white threads on their margins and hanging chandelier-like inflorescences of lily white flowers, and *Y. carnerosana,* a solitary (unbranching) species with long yellowish leaves with delicate, curling threads along their margins. Handsome plants with pale bluish leaves are the arborescent *Y. rigida* and the stemless *Y. whipplei* of the Southwest with beautiful, tall, white inflorescences. Perhaps most unusual of the yuccas

This small, compact form af *Agave victoriae-reginae* T. Moore from the slopes on the edge of the dry lake of Viesca in southwestern Coahuila, Mexico is one of the finest forms of this handsomest of species. It is hard to realize that the white stripes on the leaves do not come from an artist's brush!

Agave filifera var. *compacta* Trel. is a choice, much sought after dwarf form with short, fat, shiny dark green leaves and white paint-like markings.

is *Y. endlichiana* with short, thick, heavy, erect leaves and a tiny, inconspicuous inflorescence of purplish flowers. Some of the yuccas are quite hardy and may be grown out of doors in even quite severe climates.

Some beaucarneas, such as *B. recurvata*, make exceedingly attractive small pot plants, but they only really come into their own as massive trees with gigantic, swollen bases and heads of long, graceful leaves. The recently rediscovered oddity of the plant world, *Calibanus hookeri*, a fascinatingly homely plant (appropriately named for Shakespeare's monster, Caliban), consisting of a low, thick, rounded stem or caudex with pine-tree-like bark, and covered with tufts of grass-like leaves, is ideal for pot culture, making quite a conversation piece!

One of our greatest thrills was the rediscovery of *Calibanus hookeri* Trel.; we have since seen specimens in the wild as big as a Volkswagon! This species grows well from seed and seedlings soon develop an attractive, corky caudex.

Of the relatives of the agaves, beaucarneas with their great elephantine trunks are among the most fascinating. The forest pictured here near Tehuacan, Mexico is of *B. gracilis* Lem.

Even a small specimen of *Yucca rigida* (Engelm.) Trel. with its stiff, blue leaves is attractive.

MEXICAN CRASSULACEAE:

Among the most popular groups of succulents are the members of the stonecrop family or Crassulaceae from Mexico. These include *Echeveria, Graptopetalum, Pachyphytum* and many of the sedums. These are all generally of easy culture, the main problems being mealy bugs, nematodes and virus. In the case of mealy bugs, one must be a bit cautious as some of the crassulaceous plants are among the few which can be damaged by some of the popular pesticides such as malathion. If the infestation is not heavy, one is better off removing the pests physically or hosing them off. Nematodes can seriously impare the growth of the Mexican Crassulaceae and when serious nematode infesta-

tions are encountered one should start the plants over again from cuttings. In the case of the larger, cabbage-head echeverias, this is a good practice anyway, for as the stem grows taller, the head of leaves become smaller, as the plant is unable to support both the long stem and a large head of leaves. One can maintain larger, more spectacular plants if the heads of leaves are cut off and re-rooted each spring. Little is known about the virus which occasionally attacks the Mexican Crassulaceae and some other succulents, nor is there an effective, known cure. It appears as a sort of marbling, or mottled coloration on the leaves, and when it is detected one had better sacrifice the sick plant rather than chance infecting one's entire collection.

One of the loveliest of echeverias is *E. subrigida* (Robins. & Seat.) Rose.

ECHEVERIAS:

There are many echeveria fanciers and hybridizers, and with good reason as these charming rosette plants offer great variety of subtle coloring and texture. The hybridizers have created some striking and exceptional cultivars (or hybrids), large, showy, highly colored, ruffled plants are spectacular, but no less desirable are the pure, natural species themselves. For sheer beauty of form and color, no other succulent rivals the echeveria; the plant itself is like a beautiful flower! A sampling of echeverias might include *Echeveria subrigida*, an exquisite plant with powdery, opalescent bluish white leaves suffused with pink; *E. pulvinata* with fuzzy brown stems and rounded, succulent leaves tinged with red and covered with short, dense,

Graptopetalum filiferum (S. Wats.) Whitehead is a jewel of a plant, each tiny leaf tipped with a long hair.

This form of *Echeveria gigantea* Rose & Purpus, cv 'Scott Haselton' from Oaxaca, is one of the handsomest of the large "cabbage" type of echeveria, with pastel blue leaves edged with rose. *Sedum allantoides* Rose (right) from the border of Oaxaca and Puebla is an attractive, shrubby species with pale green leaves.

glandular hairs giving the plant a velvety texture; *E. gigantea* with giant cabbage-like heads of leaves, often of a pastel blue color, shaded with rose along the ruffled margins of the leaves; the small, clustering types, such as *E. derenbergii* or *E. elegans*, with tight rosettes of blue leaves and inflorescences of bright yellow and reddish flowers; or the thick, highly succulent, smooth jade-like leaves of *Echeveria agavoides*, its pale, yellow green leaves often marked with deep red along the margins.

Fortunately for echeveria lovers, there is the excellent, complete monographic treatment of the genus in the book *Echeveria* by Eric Walther. There are also other, popular books dealing more with the culture of these plants.

SEDUMS:

Sedum is virtually a world-wide genus, occurring in the Mediterranean region, in parts of Africa, eastern Asia and South America and nearly throughout the temperate and tropical parts of North America. It may be chauvinism on our parts, but we consider that whereas many of the old world types make excellent rockery plants, the finest collectors items come from Mexico. We are referring to such species as *Sedum morganianum*, the hanging basket plant *par excellence*, with long, graceful tassels of small, fleshy, pale, pruinose green leaves, or the outstanding arborescent types such as *S. torulosum*,

Sedum frutescens Rose is our candidate for the most exciting of the tree sedums. In its habitat, on the lava flows south of Mexico City near Cuernavaca, it grows in small pockets of dirt, and in cultivation is ill equipped to tolerate heavy soils or nematodes.

S. *oxypetalum* and S. *frutescens* which form perfect miniature trees with a stout trunk with papery bark up to six feet in height, and tiny, succulent, green leaves, or S. *craigii* with prostrate stems of large, pruinose leaves of the most delicate shade of pinkish lavender. Also choice are S. *furfuraceum* with stubby, frosted, purple-green leaves, S. *hintonii* with rounded, succulent leaves densely covered with white hairs, and S. *humifusum*, a touchy but very attractive tiny, low, creeping plant with small, lush green, densely packed, triangular leaves with tiny hairs along the margin. Most sedums are exceedingly easy to grow. Some need more specialized care, such as S. *morganianum*, the "burro's tails", a shade plant that wants generous treatment: a loose, rich soil and frequent waterings, sprayings and feedings, or the tree sedums which grow in minimal soil in the wild, usually pockets of soil in old volcanic rock, and in cultivation want a particularly loose, well-draining soil mixture; they are highly sensitive to nematodes, and if they are not doing well, one should check the roots for signs of this pest. S. *humifusum* does well if not kept too dry or in too intense light.

Of the old world sedums, some of the best are the tiny S. *multiceps* from north Africa which looks like a miniature Joshua tree, S. *sieboldii* from Japan, a fine deciduous plant for the hanging basket with gracefully arching branches of blue-gray leaves with scalloped, pink edges and terminal bouquets of pink flowers, or S. *dasyphyllum* which forms a low, dense carpet of short stems with tiny bluish leaves and relatively large white flowers.

Sedum multiceps Coss. & Dur. from Algeria is like a perfect, miniature "Joshua tree", ideal for planters or dish gardens.

Cremnophila nutans Rose (*Sedum cremnophila* Clausen) from the shaded cliffs of Tepoztlan near Cuernavaca, Mexico with rosettes of fat, pale glaucous green leaves. This genus has affinities to both *Echeveria* and *Sedum*. The other species is *Cremnophila linguaefolia* (Lem.) Moran.

Sedum furfuraceum M o r a n (left) with papillate, frosted purplish leaves is one of the most attractive of the small, shrubby sedums. The branches are twisted and sprawling with the leafy tips erect.

Kalanchoe beharensis Drake & Castillo from Madagascar, undoubtedly the largest member of the Crassulaceae forming trees at least 3 meters tall, is a most interesting plant with large, triangular leaves like elephant ears, covered with a thick, grayish felt. The form pictured here, however is Jacobsen's variety *subnuda* with nearly glabrous leaves.

Crassula pyramidalis Thunbg. (below), a remarkably symetrical species with tightly packed, triangular leaves forming square columns!

Crassula susannae Rauh & Friedr. is an exceptinally choice species whose truncate leaves have frosted, L-shaped windows.

AFRICAN CRASSULACEAE:

Members of the Crassula or "stone-crop" Family from Africa make up the heart of the average succulent collection. Many are old favorites, well deserving of their popularity, such as the lovely "panda plant", *Kalanchoe tomentosa* with felt-like silvery gray leaves marginally marked with brown, forming a small shrub about a foot high, or the "jade tree", *Crassula portulacea*, one of the most common of succulents, a bonsai-shaped, miniature tree with thick, brown, jointed stems and round, flattened, jade-like leaves. Many others are newer introductions and still collectors items, such as the remarkable little *Crassula susannae* with rosettes of leaves which are L-shaped in cross-section with frosted windows at the tips.

The main genera of African crassulaceous plants are *Crassula, Kalanchoe, Cotyledon, Adromischus, Sedum, Sempervivum* and *Aeonium.* The species of *Crassula* are varied, ranging through highly succulent types, reminiscent of the mimicry mesembs, such as *C. teres*, the "rattlesnake" plant with stems like little cones composed of tightly imbricated, scale-like leaves, *C. alstonii* or *C. cornuta* with tightly packed, silvery gray leaves, through shrubbier, rockery-types to small, arborescent types such as *C. portulacea*, or *C. arborescens* with large, round, silvery blue leaves edged with pink.

Many of the kalanchoes are weedy or vining types of little interest, but some are striking, most attractive plants for the collector, such as *K. beharensis*, the largest member of the family, with remarkable, large, felted silvery gray leaves, *K. pumila* with frosted purplish leaves and bright pink flowers or *K. gastonis-bonnieri* with gracefully recurved, powdery, chalky white leaves. The cotyledons also offer great variety from the smaller, shrubby types such as *Cotyledon ladismithensis* with fat, fuzzy green leaves to low arborescent types such as *C. paniculata* which makes a fine, miniature tree with a stout trunk and branches, peeling bark and cylindroid, succulent leaves. *C. reticulata* is one of the choicest of cotyledons with a thick, squat, branched stem and persistent, woody, much branched flower stalks which give the plant a striking appearance. *Adromischus* is an interesting group, consisting of small plants closely related to *Cotyledon*, with thick, succulent leaves with attractive shapes, coloring and patterns.

The sempervivums and aeoniums are closely related genera with dense rosettes of leaves and terminal inflorescences in which the whole stem elongates into a conical inflorescence after which that stem dies. In the case of unbranching, solitary species the plants generally then have to be started again from seed, though adventitious plantlets develop on the old, dying flower stalks. The sempervivums are stemless plants most of which offset rather profusely forming attractive, tight, little clusters. They are commonly called "hens and chickens" or "house-leeks". They are alpine succulents from the mountains of Europe, northern Asia and Africa, and consequently do not do well in extremely hot, dry climates. In temperate areas they are hardy and most attractive with shades of color through greens and purples, and occasionally with fuzzy or hairy leaves, as in the case of the lovely little *Sempervivum arachnoideum*, the heads of which seem covered with dense, fine, white cobwebs! The aeoniums come mostly from the Canary Islands and generally are low, shrubby but attractive plants, though some of the finest are stemless types such as the remarkable, absolutely flat, solitary rosettes of *Aeonium tabuliforme*. *A. nobile* is a choice species with large, solitary, cabbage-like heads of thick, pale gray green leaves. The cultivar of *A. arboreum* var. *atropurpureum*, *Aeonium* 'Swartkop' is a striking, quite spectacular plant with rosettes of shiny, dark purple-black leaves.

Cotyledon reticulata Thunbg. is a marvelous, miniature tree-like plant with persistent, branched inflorescences.

Cotyledon pearsonii Schoenl. from Namaqualand is another interesting tree-like shrub with small, linear, succulent leaves which are deciduous in our summer.

Crassula interrupta F. Mey. (left) is a pretty little plant with flat, roundish leaves covered with white hairs, particularly around the margins.

Still a fairly rare species, *Aloe laeta* Bgr. from Madagascar, with slightly glaucous leaves suffused with pinkish lavender and with closely set marginal teeth, is one of the choicest of aloes.

THE LILY FAMILY:

The lily family includes many types of intesting succulents such as the African aloes, haworthias, gasterias, the *Bowiea* or "climbing onion", and various types of bulbs, which may be considered succulent even though the succulence is generally in the bulb which is usually underground.

Aloe haworthioides Bak., a true miniature also from Madagascar, is a jewel of the genus, its thin green leaves covered and bordered with white protuberances and hairs.

ALOES:

Many aloes are large, arborescent plants which soon outgrow a potted collection, but which, in warmer areas, are ideal for landscaping. Examples of such types are *Aloe arborescens*, *A. bainesii*, *A. speciosa*, *A. marlothii* and *A. ferox*, *A. plicatilis* and *A. ramosissima*. There are numerous dwarf aloes which are perfect for pot culture. These include such gems as *Aloe haworthioides*, *A. descoingsii*, *A. aristata*, *A. jucunda*, *A. rauhii* and *A. bellatula*, to name but a few. Of the medium sized aloes, several, such as *Aloe peglerae*, *A. broomii*, *A. melanacantha*, *A. laeta* and even the common *A. striata* are well worth growing.

With the exceptions of a few of the very rare types, such as *Aloe polyphylla*, *A. haemanthifolia* and *A. dichotoma*, most aloes are exceedingly easy to cultivate, requiring no special care. The main pest to bother aloes is the aloe-mite, a tiny creature which inhabits the plant's tissues, causing monstrose, deformed growth in the leaves, stems or inflorescences. There are systemic pesticides which can eradicate aloe-mite, but unless the plant is very valuable or practically irreplaceable, one is probably better off discarding the plant as soon as aloe-mite is detected.

Fortunately, there are several excellent books on aloes, most notably Reynolds' companion works, *The Aloes of South Africa* and *The Aloes of Tropical Africa* and *Madagascar*, and *South African Aloes* by Barbara Jeppe.

One of the finest of the aloes is surely *Aloe ra-mosissima* Pill. with slender, bluish-green leaves and clusters of banana yellow flowers.

Aloe barbadensis Mill., far better known as *"Aloe vera"*, is a medicinal plant extensively cultivated for ages as a treatment for burns and other ailments or for its cosmetic values. In many parts of Mexico it has escaped from cultivation and become naturalized!

The Madagascan dwarf, *Aloe descoingsii* Reyn. is indeed a prize! . . . a clustering species with small, triangular, dark green, rough textured leaves spotted with white, and with small, bright scarlet flowers.

Another miniature species from Madagascar, only recently introduced to cultivation is *Aloe calcairophila* Reyn., a fairly touchy but highly interesting plant!

Aloe jucunda Reyn., a very neat, little, clustering species with shiny dark green leaves with whitish markings, from Somalia.

A most handsome small form of the slow grow-ing *Haworthia nigra* (Haw.) Bak. with its black-ish green leaves.

Haworthia badia v. poelln., a rare species from the Cape Province.

HAWORTHIAS:

Haworthias are the conoisseur's choice for the ideal potted collection of succulents. Var-iations in leaf shape, color, texture and pat-terning are subtle but exquisite. Haworthias seem to be either very common or exceed-ingly rare, and unfortunately the rarer types are often the choicest, most attractive and interesting plants. The reasons for their rarity are that they are usually the solitary or sel-dom offsetting types, or that all or most plants in cultivation are the same clone so the form cannot be reproduced from seed. Collectors can often obtain the clustering types such as *Haworthia variegata*, *H. limi-folia*, *H. cuspidata*, *H. reinwardtii* and some of its varieties, *H. tesselata*. Occasionally one comes across such semi-rare and choice items for sale as *H. truncata* or the similarly trun-cate *H. maughanii*, *H. setata*, *H. parksiana* or forms of *H. nigra*, but such jewels as *H. comptoniana*, *H. atrofusca*, *H. pygmaea*, etc., are rarely encountered . . . the challenge is part of the fun of haworthia collecting!

Haworthias, which come from Southern Africa, are relatively easy to grow, but to grow them well takes a bit more care and discretion. In too much shade, where they are usually relegated, they grow too lush and etiolated, that is drawn out and unnaturally elongated rather than hard and compact. In too much light they tend to look scorched and dry and virtually cease to grow. Hawor-thias put on most of their growth in the spring and fall, and when dormant in cultiva-tion may lose their roots if kept too wet or too dry, but they reroot rather easily and few plants are lost in this manner as long as one carefully tends the collection.

Haworthia reinwardtii f. *kaffirdriftensis* (G.G. Smith) Bayer, one of the most attractive forms of this variable species.

An exceptionally fine form of *Haworthia papillosa* (Salm) Haw., a species related to *H. margaritifera*.

(Below) *Haworthia asperula* Haw., a particularly fine species with rough-papillose, transparent upper leaf surfaces, giving the plant a frosted appearance.

An attractive form of the windowed *Haworthia planifolia* Haw.

Euphorbia fusca Marl., in our opinion one of the handsomest of the Medusa head type of euphorbias.

EUPHORBIAS:

No other genus of succulents exhibits the variety of form of this fabulous group of plants. The succulent euphorbias are often looked upon as the African counterpart of the American cacti, and indeed they occupy a similar ecological niche, having evolved under the same sorts of conditions. Not all euphorbias are succulent by any means and this enormous genus includes such diverse types as the poinsettia and the little garden weed known as spurge, nor are they all African, but in Africa one encounters the greatest variety among the succulent euphorbias. One can find nearly everything from tiny, inconspicuous plants smaller than a marble to great branched trees such as *Euphorbia ingens*. There are the spiney, barrel-like *E. horrida,* the tangled mass of snake-like branches arising from a single head of *E. caput-medusae,* the smooth, round, spineless, branchless *E. obesa* with a frabric-like pattern on the stem and nodes like stitching along the ribs, and hundreds of other forms which are equally different.

Among the most exciting of the euphorbias are the miniatures from Madagascar such as *E. decaryi, E. cylindrifolia* and *E. francoisii* with spiney stems tipped with rosettes of crinkled or cylindroid, succulent leaves, or the strange, flattened, mottled branches of *E. platyclada.* Madagascar also offers a wealth of fascinating, intermediate and larger forms, such as the *E. milii* or "crown of thorns" types, or the *E. neohumbertii* and *E. vigueri* group with solitary, erect, beautifully marked stems with an elegant pattern of spines along the ribs, a head of large, lush leaves and beautiful crimson to yellow flowers. The

Euphorbia virosa Willd., an attractive but highly toxic species to be treated with a healthy respect by the collector as the sap is quite poisonous.

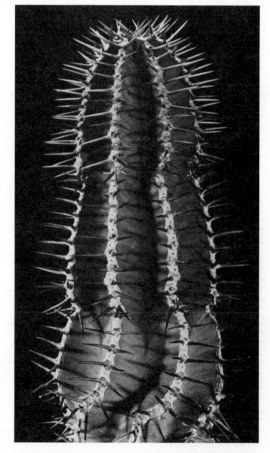

Euphorbia stellata Willd., similar to *E. squarrosa* Haw. with flattened, usually 2 angled, mottled stems arising from a thick tap root.

Euphorbia capsaintemariensis Rauh, one of the newer and one of the better of the Madagascan dwarf euphorbias.

Euphorbia aeruginosa Schweick., an exceedingly handsome species with bluish to coppery green stems and reddish brown thorn shields.

Euphorbia esculenta Marl., another excellent member of the Medusa head type, with thick, ascending, closely set branches.

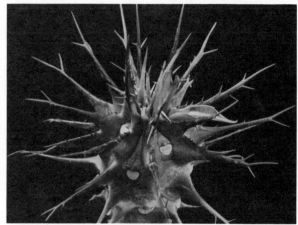

Euphorbia vigueri M. Denis, a choice and beautiful species from Madagascar with large horizontal, colorful leaves and brilliant red flowers.

Euphorbia persistens Dyer is one of our favorites, with its graceful, mottled, triangular branches arising from an enormous caudex.

Euphorbia bupleurifolia Jacq., an old favorite, remains one of the great oddities of the family, with the aspect of a pineapple or small cycad!

Madagascan euphorbias are still rare succulents, but fortunately they are currently gradually becoming available to the collector.

The euphorbias are generally of remarkably easy culture and subject to few serious pests. Most of them can take little frost, but many are ideal for landscaping in the milder parts of the country, such as Florida and coastal southern California. They are excellent for pot culture, and with a greenhouse one has a virtually unlimited selection from which to choose. There is, however, one serious problem that must be considered. Nearly all euphorbias have a more or less poisonous, milky, latex sap, and one must be exceedingly cautious in handling and propagating these plants. If a plant is wounded, and one gets the milky sap on one's fingers, one should immediately wash one's hands before the sap gets rubbed into the eyes, mouth or some cut. Fortunately for the collector, there is another attractive little succulent which is the antidote for euphorbia-poison, the small, shrubby *Aeonium lindleyi* from the Canary Islands. A euphorbia collector should always have a plant of this aeonium in his collection. If one gets euphorbia sap into the mouth or eyes, the juice of a leaf of *A. lindleyi* stops the burning almost immediately. We do not mean to frighten collectors away from the wonderful euphorbias, but only to caution them against the very real dangers involved with careless handling of the plants.

The four-angled *Euphorbia resinifera* Bgr. from Morocco forms with age great cushion-like clusters.

Euphorbia platyclada Rauh (below) is a most peculiar, intriguing species from Madagascar with flattened, mottled stems.

Euphorbia decidua Bally & Leach, an interesting rarity with deciduous branches.

Euphorbia pulvinata Marl., a very attractive, clustering species.

Euphorbia bougheyi Leach, a delicate, tender, tropical species with graceful, leaf-like branches.

Euphorbia cryptospinosa Bally, a most unusual species with fluted, brownish purple stems and bright red flowers which looks more like a peniocereus or wilcoxia than a euphorbia!

Euphorbia globosa (Haw.) Sims, a charming species with globular, branching joints.

Monadenium schubei (Pax) N.E. Br., a member of a fascinating genus closely related to *Euphorbia*.

Conophytum wittebergense de Boer with its intricate pattern of lines and windows is one of the most desirable species of this interesting genus. *Conophytum breve* var. *minutiflorum* (Schwantes) Rawe (right) with smooth, glaucous bodies like rounded pebbles, and yellow flowers (photo R. Rawe).

THE MIMICRY MESEMBS:

The mimicry mesembs, from South Africa, are an absolutely fascinating group of succulents, most of which, however, require fairly specialized care. Each "body" mainly consists of a pair of highly succulent, rounded leaves which seasonally are replaced by a new pair. Normally, during periods of growth one would expect it to be necessary to water a plant more heavily. This is not necessarily true with these plants, for, to avoid rupturing the old leaves through sudden growth, the process of replacement must be a slow one, and after all, the plants have an adequate reservoir of water stored in their leaves to carry them through this part of their growth cycle. With the highly succulent or "stemless" mesembs, the old precaution often applied to succulent plants is particularly applicable: "when in doubt, don't water!" To collectors inexperienced in growing mesembs, we generally recommend that they not water until they see visible signs of shriveling in the leaves. This type of mesemb seems better able to take complete drying out of the roots than can most other types of succulent plants.

Pleiospilos species, such as the "split rocks", *P. nelii* and *P. bolusii* are old favorites which do quite well for everyone, provided they are not kept too wet. Their angular or rounded, brownish gray leaves speckled with pinhole windows are more like chips of granite than living plants. The flowers are large and bright yellow, opening each afternoon for several days and becoming successively more orange in color as the flower ages.

Lithops is probably the most popular group of mesembs among collectors, and all species are truly charmers with small, rounded, subtly colored pairs of leaves, patterned with darker, windowed areaes. The flowers are large and

bright yellow or white. Such small "stemless" mesembs are tasty prey to birds, but we have found that a top-dressing of rounded pebbles, colored similarly to the plants, is not only intriguing in that it accentuates the mimicry nature of the lithops, but it is effective and natural camouflage against the predation of birds!

Conophytum is one of the most demanding genera of mesembs in its specific requirements and a long period of dormancy is quite essential. Most successful cultivators of conophytums leave the plants completely dry for about nine months of the year, beginning

Aloinopsis schoonesii L. Bolus, often called "nananthus", is a charming mesemb with dark green leaves spotted with pin hole windows.

Trichodiadema species, such as *T. densum* (Haw.) Schwantes (left) and *T. bulbosum* (Haw.) Schwantes (right) may be cultivated to expose their interesting swollen roots and trained into attractive bonsai-like shapes.

watering only in August or late July and withholding it after October or mid-November. The plants, with tiny little round, bluish or greenish bodies, sometimes patterned with darker windowed areas, soon form miniature clusters of many heads. During the dormant period the skins become dry and papery, and it's very hard for a loving collector to withhold water from these plants, but then in mid-summer the small but very pretty flowers start to break through the dried sheaths of the old skins, and the plants seem to come alive again.

There are many other fascinating groups of mesembs: *Fenestraria* or "baby toes", *Lapidaria*, the beautifully textured species of *Gibbaeum*, the rare *Muiria*, etc., all of which are delightful plants to cultivate, even if, from time to time, one ends up with a little pile of mush where the day before a plant had been. Other shrubbier mesembs have a great deal to offer too, and are far easier culturewise, such as *Faucaria*, or "tiger jaws" or the species of *Trichodiadema* with spine-tipped leaves and great, tuberous roots. There are various books specializing on the culture of mesembs, but one of the most beautiful and fascinating of all books on succulent plants is Herre's marvelous *Genera of the Mesembryanthemaceae* with colored paintings and information about every genus of this large family.

One of the loveliest of the mesembs is *Gibbaeum album* N.E. Br. with white, velvety textured leaves and white flowers. Among the great oddities of the family are the various species of *Monilaria* (right) with soft, cylindroid leaves and jointed stems like beads on a necklace.

Caralluma penicillata (Defl.) N.E. Br. from southern Arabia forms shrubs up to 3 feet tall with erect, four-angled, light green stems and heads of small star-shaped flowers.

Caralluma solenophora Lav. (below) from S.W. Arabia is a shy bloomer but the flowers are attractive, the corolla lobes tipped with vibratile hairs.

THE MILKWEED FAMILY:

Few plants offer such incredibly intricate and exquisite flowers of such variation in color and texture as do the succulent asclepiads, members of the milkweed family. Of the hundreds of succulent species in this large family, some are hardy types and will do well in any collection, many are difficult species requiring specialized attention, but the majority will do well with reasonable care. For a representative collection of the succulent asclepiads, a warm, dry greenhouse is a virtual necessity.

THE STAPELIADS:

In "stapeliads" one includes the genera *Stapelia, Caralluma, Huernia, Piaranthus, Echidnopsis, Stapelianthus,* and a variety of stapelia-like plants most of which are from Africa and Southwestern Asia. They are generally creeping to erect plants with four-angled to rounded stems which root and off-set at the basal nodes, with five-pointed, carrion flowers, most of which resemble various types of meat or flesh in color, texture and odor, as they rely on flies as the chief pollinator. All this hardly sounds inviting, but even while one may be repelled, one can hardly help but be intrigued by the strange beauty of the flowers: the corollas covered with brown, black, purple or snow white hairs, or fringed with a margin of vibratile hairs that stir in the slightest breath of air; the wrinkled, mottled, speckled or swollen corollas in shades of red, orange, brown, purple, yellow or green, such as the remarkable, Persian-carpet-like flower of *Edithcolea,* the red-velvet flowers of *Caralluma socotrana* or the great spheres of black flowers of *Caralluma speciosa!*

Caralluma dodsoniana Lav. from Somalia is one of the most curious of recent discoveries with its wrinkled, brownish stems and dark brown flowers.

Among the easier species we would recommend for the beginner, the old favorite, *Stapelia variegata* with its mottled stems and wrinkled, yellowish flowers speckled with purple, *S. gigantea* or *S. nobilis* with their astonishingly large flowers, up to a foot in diameter, of a light yellowish tan color, transversely striped with narrow crimson lines, or *S. hirsuta* with its felted stems and flowers covered with soft purplish hairs. Success with these usually induces one to try some of the rarer, more difficult types.

Stapeliads are heavy feeders so they want a reasonably large container, a fairly rich but well-draining potting mix, and liberal watering except in the dormant season. We have had the most success in leaving our stapeliads nearly completely dry throughout the winter months, from, say, November to March. The plants, during this period, look weak and floppy and miserable, but soon after the first watering in the spring they nearly snap back to life. Most stapeliads are easily propagated by simply removing a branch or two; in fact, we would recommend starting your collection over through such propagation every year or so, as most stapeliads grow fairly rank and flower only from the new growth.

Among the more unusual, even outlandish types are *Hoodia* with large, saucer-like flowers and robust, euphorbia-like stems, *Trichocaulon* and the exceedingly rare *Pseudolithos* which resemble lumps of rock rather than any living plant!

Hoodias are among the most amazing of the stapeliads for their strikingly large, often saucer-shaped flowers. The flowers of *Hoodia currori* (Hook.) Decne, pictured here, are particularly hairy and distinctly 5-lobed.

Huernia quinta (Phillips) Wh. & Sl., a charming species with pert flowers striped with dark lavender bands.

Caralluma aaronsis (Hart.) N.E. Br. from Israel and Jordan.

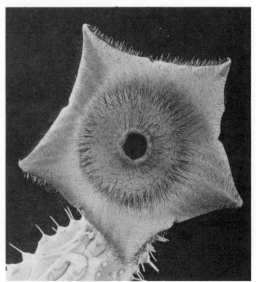

Caralluma maculata var. *brevidens* H. Huber, better known as "rangeana".

Ceropegia woodii Schltr., the "rosary vine", an old favorite.

Pseudolithos horwoodii Bally & Lav. from Somalia.

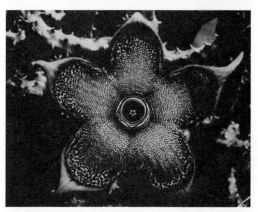

Edithcolea grandis N.E. Br. with a flower patterned like a Persian carpet.

RELATIVES OF THE STAPELIADS:

Related to the stapeliads, and equally fascinating, are varous groups such as *Ceropegia*, vine-like, trailing stems, generally arising from small, potato-like tubers with intricate, little, vase-like flowers, *Cynanchum*, most notably the recently described *C. marnierianum* from Madagascar, with its wrinkled, twig-like, brownish purple stems with gouty, swollen nodes, and little, yellow cage-like flowers, and *Brachystelma*, tuberous plants with short, leafy or vining stems and huernia to ceropegia-like flowers. *Ceropegia woodii* (the "Rosary Vine") is the most common of the ceropegias, but equally interesting are such types as *C. ampliata*, *C. haygarthii*, *C. stapeliiformis* and many others, all with unique, incredibly intricate flowers. *C. dichotoma* is different in that it is a small shrub with terete, upright stems, rather than trailing, vine-like stems. *Brachystelma barberae* has perhaps the most remarkable and the most putrid inflorescences, great bouquets of purplish flowers with the tips of the slender corolla lobes connate, joined together like miniature bird cages. Whereas most ceropegias and cynanchums are of easy culture, the brachystelmas with their large, succulent tubers are a bit more touchy and one must be careful to provide extra good drainage and not to over-water.

Brachystelma barberae Harv. ex Hook.

Othonna cacalioides L.f., one of the daintiest and most intriguing of the miniature othonnas with its tiny flowers and rounded, truncated stems which are leafless in summer.

(Above left): a probably as yet undescribed species of *Senecio* with thick, speckled stems and dark markings radiating from the nodes.

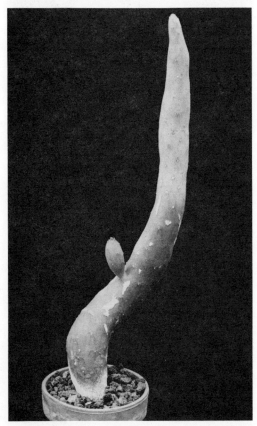

Senecio deflersii Schwarz, a most singular, highly succulent species with rounded, bright, light green stems and yellow flowers, from S. Arabia.

SUCCULENTS OF THE DAISY FAMILY:

The main succulent groups in the daisy family, or Compositae, are the othonnas and senecios and they occur mostly in Africa. There is an interesting arborescent, somewhat succulent senecio in Mexico, the "palo loco", *Senecio praecox*, so named because the terminal clusters of flowers appear before the leaves reappear, that is, prematurely. There is also a succulent member of the genus *Coreopsis* which occurs along the coastal region of California, *Coreopsis gigantea*, which in the dry summer season look like a lot of dead roots stuck upside-down into the ground, but which each winter are covered with airy, green foliage and large yellow flowers.

Of the two main groups of succulent daisies, the senecios are more common in collections, represented by such oddities as the "inch worm", *Senecio pendulus*, a mottled purplish stemmed, virtually leafless plant which arches back to the ground, roots again and arches out in another loop; S. *fulgens* with gnarled, tuberous roots and stems with rosettes of glaucous blue leaves and deep orange flowers, or S. *scaposus*, an elegant but touchy plant with rosettes of cylindroid leaves completely clothed with a cobwebby white felt. Undoubtedly the most popular senecio is the "string of pearls", *Senecio rowleyanus*, which makes a marvelous hanging

A unique crested form of *Senecio gregorii* (S. Moore) Jacobs. which in its normal form has erect, thin, rounded, pencil-like stems.

Othonna retrorsa DC. from Little Namaqualand in the Cape, S. Africa.

Othonna lepidocaulis Schltr., also from Little Namaqualand in the Cape.

Senecio pendulus (Forsk.) Sch. Bip. from S. Arabia, Ethiopia and Somalia.

basket plant with long, thin, string-like stems bearing little, rounded, windowed, green leaves.

Other than a few othonnas that have been around for years, most of this genus are fairly new to collectors in this country. As opposed to the senecios which are generally of very easy culture, the othonnas mostly need specialized care. They are winter growers, and if allowed or forced to grow all year long, they won't be around for long. They are mostly leafy succulents, and when the leaves start to dry out it is a sign that they are ready to go dormant and all water should be withheld until the fall when the first signs of new growth become evident. Among the more interesting othonnas are *Othonna herrei* with strangely knobby, brown stems and yellow flowers, *O. retrorsa* with stems densely covered with the dried remains of the persistent, pale blue, thin, spathulate leaves, or *O. lepidocaulis* with stems covered with yellowish, scale-like leaf bases giving it the appearance of the foot of a chicken! One of the very best is *O. cacalioides*, better known under the synonymous names of *O. minima* or *O. pygmaea*, with little, rounded, potato-like stems, bearing tufts of deciduous, thin, bluish, spathulate leaves and the tiniest of flowers on exceedingly long, thin stalks, a little jewel of a plant which must be allowed a long and complete rest period if it is to survive.

Fouquieria purpusii Brandegee, one of the fascinating barrel trees of southern Mexico in the Ocotillo Family with a bluish green stem marked with lines of gray bark.

THE EXOTICS:

An entire book, or rather several books could (and should) be written on the subject of the more exotic succulents. These rare and unusual types have only in the last decade come into their own among collectors. Their number includes caudiciform and semisucculent arborescent forms such as the fabulous pachypodiums of the Oleander Family, the succulent adenias of the Passion-flower Family, *Bursera* and *Commiphora* species such as the "elephant trees" of the Frankincense Family, dioscoreas, with caudices (or tuber-like bodies) like the carapice of a tortoise, of the Yam Family, the monstrous, swollen stemmed cyphostemmas of the Grape Family and the fantastic succulent fouquierias of the Ocotillo Family such as the boojum tree or "idria" of Baja California and the barrel trees of Mexico with blue-green bark, *Fouquieria purpusii* and *F. fasciculata.*

A forest of *Pachypodium lamerei* and didiereas growing in the Madagascan succulent house at the botanical garden of Heidelberg.

A small plant of *Pachypodium brevicaule* with bright yellow flowers, from Madagascar.

Few plants offer greater interest to the horticulturist than the various species of *Pachypodium,* whether *P. brevicaule* with its exceedingly truncated, almost flattened, bulging, bumpy, knobby trunk with tufts of green leaves and long stemmed, canary-yellow flowers, *P. geayi* or *P. lamerei* with tall, straight, swollen trunks covered with spines and with a terminal rosette of long, slender, gracefully curving leaves, or the shrubby *P. succulentum* with a large, swollen, underground caudex and delicate, pink, pin-wheel shaped flowers. The pachypodiums take generous succulent care: warmth, a rich, well-draining soil, generous watering except in the dormant season and bright light. Perhaps the oddest of the pachypodiums is the slow-growing *P. namaquanum* with a thick trunk and long, deflexed spines and a crown of short, crinkly, slightly fuzzy leaves. In its habitat it is considered a haunted plant by the natives, and one can well imagine the eery quality of a hillside covered with an army of these strange creatures called "ghost mens" or "half mens"!

A fine, small specimen of the "elephant tree", *Pachycormus discolor* (Benth.) Coville from Baja California (note the small, succulent dorstenia growing at its base!). *Pachypodium succulentum* (L.f.) A. DC. (left) from the Cape, S. Africa.

All it takes to cultivate the finest dwarf "elephant trees" or "incense trees" is an aesthetically pleasingly shaped plant to start with and an artistic eye for thinning, pruning and training to keep and accentuate the natural shape under the more generous conditions of cultivation. Such a fine specimen of, say, *Bursera fagaroides*, an African *Commiphora*, or *Pachycormus discolor* of the Cashew Family, would appeal to almost every plantsperson, from beginning collector to bonsai specialist! And what could be less demanding in its cultural requirements; it does not need or want to be watered daily, as do the traditional bonsais, and it can even be left dry for extended periods and survive. One does not want to push the dwarf tree type succulents, for it is their slow growth that creates the perfect, miniature quality. New, lush growth should regularly be "pinched back" to the first or second bud on the branch.

Adenia glauca Schinz, also from the Cape Province, one of several interesting, succulent species of the Passion Flower Family. On this specimen the long, clambering stems are pruned back, and the cuttings may be rooted and will slowly develop the swollen, succulent caudex.

An exceedingly large specimen of *Dioscorea* (*Testudinaria*) *elephantipes* (L'Her.) Engl. along with a tall *Pachypodium geayi* and various euphorbias in one of our succulent houses.

One of the all-time oddities of the succulent plant world is *Dioscorea* (or *Testudinaria*) *elephantipes*, the "elephant's foot" plant from Africa, with an enormous, fissured, barky caudex and slender, vining, leafy branches, a marvel of the plant world, or its more recently popular Mexican relation, *Dioscorea macrostachya* with a more flattened caudex. The dioscoreas grow well and relatively fast to an interesting size from seed, though it takes years to grow the enormous, most impressive specimens.

❋   ❋   ❋

A marvelous group of exotic succulents is the Didiereaceae from Madagascar with such unusual plants as *Didierea trollii* and *D. madagascariensis, Alluaudia procera, A. ascendens, A. montagnacii, A. dumosa, A. comosa, A. humbertii, Alluaudiopsis fiherensis* and *A. marnieriana*, all intriguing plants with spiny, woody, starkly erect or clambering stems. Their culture is easy. They need warmth in winter, but otherwise, when in leaf and not dormant, they can take generous treatment.

❋   ❋   ❋

Adenia pechuelii (Engl.) Harms from S.W. Africa, one of the rarest and most unusual of the genus.

There are three main types of succulent grapes, members of the Vitaceae: the vining types with thin, round, woody stems, the clambering types with flattened or angular, jointed, succulent stems, and the marvelous cyphostemmas, with enormously thickened succulent caudices and papery bark. The vining types are typified by *Cissus tuberosa* from Mexico with leafy stems which arise from a large, round, basal swelling, and where the stems touch the ground, they root and form other similar swellings. Of the jointed types, *Cissus quadrangularis*, also called *C. cactiformis*, is typical with its square, four-angled stems (there is a five angled form from Somalia called tongue twistingly *C. quinquangularis!*). An outstanding species of this type is *Cissus subaphylla* from Socotra with flattened, glaucous blue, long, oval, jointed stems.

Those marvels of the succulent plant world, the cyphostemmas, were generally included in the genus *Cissus* but have recently been segregated into the genus *Cyphostemma*. Some, such as *C. cramerana*, are giants with great, swollen trunks up to 12 feet tall, others, such as *C. juttae* or *C. bainesii*, the height of a person, and still others have low, fat, knobby caudices such as *C. seitziana* with leaves covered with white felt, *C. uter* or *C. betiformis*. All are fascinating plants well worth cultivating.

Decaryia madagascariensis Choux, the "zig-zag plant" from Madagascar.

Cissus tuberosa DC., a succulent grape from Mexico which in the growing season produces a long, leafy vine which roots at the nodes.

Ficus palmeri S. Wats., a succulent member of the Fig Family from Mexico.

Plumeria acutifolia Poir. (= *P. acuminata* Ait.), the "frangipani", a relative of the pachypodium in the Oleander Family, in the dormant state.

The coral-red fruit of *Cyphostemma bainesii* (Hook.f.) B. Desc. from S.W. Africa, a succulent grape which develops a thick trunk to 6 feet tall!

THE LONELY SUCCULENT COLLECTOR:

Many who have newly discovered the fascinating world of cacti and other succulents feel that they are entirely alone in their new-found passion. You have bought a few plants, but can find little information on their care or their classification, neither in the libraries nor in the local bookstores. You try to share your hobby with your family or friends, but every time you mention your plant collection they look at you as if you had lost your mind! You would like to enlarge your collection, but there is a limited selection in your super-market, department store or even local nursery.

Believe us; you're not alone! In the United States there is a cactus and succulent society with about 5,000 members and with smaller, affiliated clubs throughout the country. In the world there are over 60 publications specializing in succulent plants, and hundreds of cactus and succulent societies. In the Cactus and Succulent Journal you can find names and addresses of local clubs, of dealers specializing in succulent plants and books dealing with cacti and other succulents, and a "Round Robin" club for members of the Cactus & Succulent Society of America which offers the opportunity to correspond by letter with other collectors throughout the world who share the same interests.

Seyrigia humbertii Keraudren, a strange, succulent member of the Cucumber Family with swollen, potato-like roots and long, slender, clambering stems clothed in fuzzy, white felt, from Madagascar. Note the flower on the lower part of the stem on the right!

Ceraria pygmaea (Pill.) Pill. from Little Namaqualand in the Cape, S. Africa, a marvelous, miniature member of the Portulaca Family.

A FINAL WORD

We have avoided trying to give *rules* in this essay, and this approach will probably be frustrating to many of you. There is the illusion of comfort in rules such as "water when dry" (what is "dry"?), "full sun" (California sun or New York sun?), "water every two weeks" (irregardless of pot size and porosity, humidity, activity of growth, size and habit of plant, etc.?). There are no rules concerning good culture which may not and occasionally should not be broken; there are principles and guide-lines which when followed with interest, common sense and love will be of help. If the culture of plants were a cut-and-dried matter rather than a living experience, it would have far less to offer. Fortunately such is not the case, and the love of and involvement with plants can be a never-ending source of enjoyment and education.

Kalanchoe gastonis-bonnieri Hamet & Perr. with graceful, powdery white leaves.

Cotyledon orbiculata var. *oophylla* Dtr. from Great Namaqualand in S.W. Africa.

Crassula marchandii Friedr., known under the nomen nudum, *Crassula* "otzenii".

Peperomia columella Rauh & P.C. Hutch., a charming, windowed member of the Piperaceae from Peru.

Crassula teres Marl., the "rattlesnake" plant.